CW00541372

Tango Stories: Musical Secrets

Tango Stories: Musical Secrets

Michael Lavocah

milonga press

Published in Great Britain by milonga press

milonga press
33 Britannia Road
Norwich NR1 4HP
England
www.milonga.co.uk

First published 2012
Reprinted with corrections 2013

A CIP catalogue record for this book is available from the British Library

Hardback: ISBN 978-0-9573276-0-3
Paperback: ISBN 978-0-9573276-1-0

Edited by Mike Stocks
Cover design by Nigel Orme

Printed in the UK by MPG-Biddles

Printed on paper sourced from responsibly managed and sustainable forests

set in Garamond 11/14

La música me lleva

(The music leads me)

- Tete (Pedro Rusconi)

About this book

This is a book of stories.

I loved tango music from the first moment I heard it. As I slowly learnt how to listen to it, I came to deeply appreciate the musicians who created it.

At the beginning there were no arrangements. The music was played *a la parilla*, "on the grill" – two or three musicians improvising their own parts from music which, if it was written down at all, consisted of melody and bass lines.

As the music became more sophisticated it retained this personal stamp. All the bands had arrangers, but they wrote their arrangements around the individual musicians who were going to perform them. Even more than the arrangers, it was the musicians themselves who drove the development of the musical form.

So when you hear Troilo's pianist go crazy, that is not just any pianist, that is Orlando Goñi. That bandoneón variation from Pugliese is the work of Osvaldo Ruggiero, and no-one else, whilst the agitated, unpredictable piano in the D'Arienzo orchestra is Rodolfo Biagi. All of this is not to mention the unmistakeable piano of Pugliese himself, or of Carlos Di Sarli, or the bandoneón of Troilo. All of them imprinted their unique stamp on the music they created, and were irreplaceable. This is art, when you can recognise a musician from just a few notes.

These musicians are personalities with their own stories and history, and the tangos they performed have their stories too. Accordingly this is a book of stories. They are not my stories; they are our stories, and I pass them on to you in the hope that they will help you open your ears to this incredible music. From the ear to the heart, and from the heart to the feet.

So much of what is called 'dance music' in the Western world today isn't dance music in the former sense of the phrase. There is plenty of music created as a backdrop to dance, but when we say dance music we mean something else: music that has co-evolved with the dance that it is designed for, the two strands interlocked like DNA. By the same token, we no longer know how to listen to music in the way people once did. Listen with your bodies, listen with your feet, listen with your heart. Listen with every cell of your body. Listen with your spirit.

I hope this book will help you on this journey.

Michael Lavocah

Istanbul, New Year's Eve, 2011

My thanks to Ruth Zimmermann
who first encouraged me to tell these stories
and gave me a space in which to do it

Preface

The enforced migration of Africans into brutal slavery in the Americas in the 16th to 19th centuries had a wholly unforeseen consequence: the cross-pollination of the musical culture of America and Europe with that of Africa. This fertilization gave rise to the three great musics of the 20th century.

In North America, the result was blues, jazz and swing.

In the Caribbean, it produced (amongst other rhythms) the *son montuno*, from which developed *mambo* and later *salsa*.

In Argentina, it was the tango.

The conditions which created the tango were unique and will never be repeated. Millions of displaced Europeans from many nations arrived in a new world on the other side of the globe. Cut off from their homeland, lacking a common history and culture, even a common language, they were thrown together into the melting pot. The result: tango.

Tango is the ultimate world music.

How to use this book

Dear reader, you and I are not sitting together and I don't have the chance to play a track to you and exclaim: *There! Did you hear what the piano just did?*

However, thanks to the digital age, we have the next best thing. Visit the book's website:

www.tangomusicsecrets.com

and you'll find some links to playlists on an on-line listening service, Spotify. Each chapter has a separate playlist. When a song we are talking about is on the playlist, this symbol appears in the margin:

These lists are not my lists of the "best" music from each orchestra: they are selected to help you understand the sound of an orchestra and the contribution of its members. Not everything I'd like to play you is online, nor is the version of a particular recording that's available online necessarily the best one.

At the end of the chapter I make recommendations for which CD to buy. I try not to taunt you with music that's not available, but there is still plenty of important tango music that is not available to buy, even from some of the big orchestras.

Terminology:

- track titles appear in quotation marks, and unless we are just skipping over them, in bold, like this: "**La cumparsita**".
- With track titles, we use the abbreviation (m) for milonga and (v) for vals.
- album titles in the text are in single quotes: 'Epoca de oro'.
- Argentine words that you may not be familiar with appear in italics, like this: *canyengue*. I explain them where I can; otherwise, check the glossary at the end of the book.

Contents

Part 1

An introduction to the orchestras

Tango historians talk about a Golden Age of tango lasting forty years with its high point being the Golden Decade of the 1940s. At that time there were a lot of tango orchestras in Buenos Aires: perhaps a couple of hundred. Today, a tango DJ would be able to name a couple of dozen. But which are the most important?

Everyone has their own list, so here is my "big four": D'Arienzo, Di Sarli, Troilo, and Pugliese. These are the most important for the tango dancer. Not only are they great to dance to; these orchestras shaped tango history.

Then we have a second tier – orchestras which are also musically important, perhaps as successful as those in the first list, but not making it into the top four: Canaro, Caló, Lomuto, Firpo, Láurenz, D'Agostino, Tanturi, Demare, De Angelis, Fresedo, Biagi, Donato, Rodríguez, De Caro, the Típica Victor… it's a long list!

Then there will be a third tier – by no means third rate. These are orchestras which made fine music but were unsuccessful (Minotto, Petrucelli), or were perhaps not so innovative (Malerba, José García), or which were too innovative (Salgán, Francini-Pontier) or which simply started too late to be truly great dance orchestras (Varela, Domingo Federico). And finally there are the ones that no-one much likes nowadays, such as Sassone and Maderna.

The most prolific tango orchestra was that of Canaro. Why isn't he in my top four? The answer lies not so much in where you draw the line – I could easily have decided to have a top five – but when. Canaro's importance lies before the 1940s so unfortunately he gets relegated to the second division. Had we been looking in the mid 1930s he would definitely have merited a place at the top.

We aren't going to talk about all the orchestras in this book – only the ones you'll hear when you go out dancing. We must start by getting a handle on the Big Four because they are the reference points for understanding all the others. And any discussion of them must start with the King of The Beat himself, Juan D'Arienzo.

1 / Juan D'Arienzo: The King of the Beat

Listening guide

ORQUESTA
JUAN D'ARIENZO

piano - **Lidio Fasoli**:
1/Hotel Victoria (1935)
2/ Pabellón de las rosas (v) (1936)

piano - **Rodolfo Biagi**:
3/Nueve de julio (1935) 4/Rawson (1936)
5/El choclo (1937) 6/Silueta porteña (m) (1936)
7/Pensalo bien * (1938)

piano - **Antonio Polito**:
8/Nada más * (1938) 9/Felicia (1939)

* estribillo: **Alberto Echagüe**

Note: Over his long career D'Arienzo recorded most of his big hits several times, often decades apart. You can't assume that a recording is the one meant just because it has the same name – you need to check the year, but often it is not given. Eventually you learn to tell from the sound.

From this list, "Hotel Victoria", "9 de julio" and "Nada más" were recorded three times and "El choclo" four. (The later versions of "Hotel Victoria" were recorded as "Gran Hotel Victoria", but you can't rely on the record companies to get this right).

Who is Juan D'Arienzo? This is the man who almost single-handedly propelled an entire city to its feet, turning a generation of tango listeners into tango dancers. It was a revolution.

D'Arienzo paved the way for all the dance orchestras who came after him in the 1940s. You could even say that he prepared the ground for the Golden Decade of the 1940s itself. D'Arienzo does not inaugurate the Golden Age, but without him it is unthinkable. Tango would simply not exist in the way it does today, and an army of modern aficionados would have to find something else to do with their time. He changed history – not just musical history, but social history as well.

The D'Arienzo formula was simple. Turning his back on a decade of musical evolution, he returned to the repertoire and in a way to the style of the *guardia vieja* (the old guard) but with more modern arrangements and an irresistible staccato edge to his beat. The intelligentsia were scandalised – even today, tango intellectuals denigrate his music – but the public loved it, and he was christened *El Rey del Compás* – The King of the Beat.

Now, the D'Arienzo orchestra was not born fully formed. There was one more key element in the D'Arienzo story: his pianist Rodolfo Biagi. It was a match made in heaven. But Biagi was not the first pianist in the D'Arienzo orchestra: no, that was **Lidio Fasoli**. A great place to start with D'Arienzo is to listen to the band's 1935 recording of "**Hotel Victoria**", recorded at their very first recording session in July 1935. Fasoli is on piano and the tango chugs along with a strong 4x8 *marcato*, which you can count out like this: "**1** and **2** and **3** and **4** and". It has a good pulse (*compás*) but doesn't quite have the excitement that we normally associate with the orchestra.

D'Arienzo used to play at the cabaret Chantecler, where Biagi – recently returned from an overseas tour – was a frequent patron. One day Fasoli was late for work once too often and Biagi was offered the empty chair. He didn't need to be asked twice.

Like any good bandleader, D'Arienzo had strong ideas about how he wanted his musicians to play. One more quirk of fate was required before Biagi was able to work his magic on the D'Arienzo sound.

D'Arienzo himself would often arrive late for performances and the band would warm up without him. On one such occasion Biagi decided to let rip and play "**9 de julio**" *his* way. The Biagi style was more rhythmic, more aggressive even, than what had gone before. The public went mad for it and D'Arienzo was forced to adopt the new style. From then on the success of the band, and of tango itself as a popular art form, was assured.

D'Arienzo cut his first sides with Biagi at the piano on the very last day of 1935. They were the vals "**Orillas del plata**" and, most appropriately, "**9 de julio**". People often ask me if Biagi is playing on a particular D'Arienzo side. You can hear the difference between Fasoli and Biagi once you know what to listen for. In the spaces between musical phrases, Biagi inserts very short, staccato interventions that have a nervous feeling about them, adding a lot of energy to the music. Biagi's playing is, well, a bit shy on "**9 de julio**" but fast forward two years to "**El choclo**" (1937) and his characteristic fills can be heard very clearly as early as the second bar of music. They don't so much join the phrases together as punctuate them. The arrangement is super staccato: listen closely to the opening bars and you can hear that it's not only the bandoneóns that are playing staccato, it's the violins as well.

In 1936's "**Rawson**" there is something else going on rhythmically, right at the beginning of the piece: strong syncopations (beats in unexpected places) that to a dancer are strongly suggestive of the *corte* or cut step. Listen to the piece and you'll notice that these syncopations always occur in groups of three. This knowledge really helps the dancer to interpret the music.

2 x 4 (2 by 4, or "dos por cuatro")

It's often said that D'Arienzo returned to the 2 x 4 rhythm, but what does this mean?

Take two beats ('2') and divide each in half, and you'd have four quarter notes ('4'), a bit like slicing a cake in four. That's 2 x 4, but in tango we mean something else. The first beat is not divided equally, so the first slice of cake gets bigger (⅜ instead of ¼) at the expense of the second (⅛ instead of ¼). This is shown by the dot next to the first note:

In case this doesn't make any sense, let's write the same thing down using numbers. Because we're now talking about eighths we'll need 8 numbers to cover the bar of music. The bold notes are the ones with emphasis:

1 2 3 **4 5** 6 **7** 8 – or **1** x x **4 5** x **7** x – sounds like this: **1** (pause) **and 2, and**

This is the rhythm of the early tango and it's the same rhythm used in the habanera, and in milonga. The unequal division of the first beat, a kind of syncopation, creates a choppiness to the rhythm.

The next step was to simply divide the cake into eight. Now we've got the 4x8:

1 2 **3** 4 **5** 6 **7** 8 – sounds like this: 1 and 2 and 3 and 4 and

The choppiness of the syncopation is gone, so everything sounds smoother, although one is free to add syncopation (change the emphasis) anywhere one wishes. This happens as early as 1916. Confusingly, all this music was also written with a 2 x 4 time signature.

The next development comes from De Caro in 1924: just get rid of the numbers which aren't in bold and re-number:

1 2 3 4

This is the 4 x 4. It allows phrases to be longer and hence more expressive but the choppy energy of the 2 x 4 is completely gone. D'Arienzo doesn't really return to the 2 x 4 at all, but to its more sophisticated brother, the 4 x 8. This music was written with a 2 x 4 time signature and is still referred to in tango circles as 2 x 4.

Biagi's fills are very obvious in "**9 de julio**" and "**Rawson**". Now let's try a slightly less obvious example: the iconic "**Pensalo bien**" ("Think it over") (1938), where you can hear the same thing happening but just a bit more gently.

Unfortunately this number, recorded in June 1938, was the last they recorded together. What happened? The story goes that one evening the band were playing the vals "**Lágrimas y sonrisas**" and Biagi was just on fire. The audience applauded him wildly, refusing to stop until Biagi made a small bow from his seat. At this point, D'Arienzo walked over, leant down and whispered in Biagi's ear: *"I'm the only star of this orchestra. You're fired."*[1]

D'Arienzo recruited Juan Polito to fill the empty chair but they soon found that the Biagi style was more difficult than it sounded. In D'Arienzo's own words, in an interview given in 1975: "The foundation of my orchestra is the piano. I regard it as irreplaceable." Polito eventually managed to make a fair imitation of his style but you can hear that what he is playing is scripted by the arranger. In comparison, Biagi's playing is wild and unpredictable. A nice example of the post-Biagi orchestra is the 1939 instrumental "**Felicia**". The compás has intensified greatly since the 1935 "**Hotel Victoria**" and the piece has great drive, even without Biagi.

How popular was Juan D'Arienzo?

D'Arienzo was by any measure the most popular orchestra of the Golden Age. He sold the most records and his musicians received the highest pay – more than those of Troilo, Di Sarli and Canaro.

RCA Victor couldn't produce his records fast enough. Record shops marked up his discs *above* list price and sometimes refused to sell you a D'Arienzo disc unless you bought something else as well. His recordings of "**La cumparsita**" have sold 14 million copies.

---

[1] http://www.tangoandchaos.org/comments_updates_new.htm [Accessed: 29th June 2012]

How to listen to D'Arienzo

The bandoneóns

D'Arienzo's orchestra is a rhythm machine, and if the axis of that engine is the piano, then the moving parts – the pistons – are a line-up of five bandoneóns and five violins, one more than the usual four. D'Arienzo was famous for his bandoneón section and they are the driving force in his orchestra. They maintain the *compás* throughout with lots of rhythmic play and fabulous *variaciones* – the variations that form the final climax of many tango arrangements.

The violin

The importance of the bandoneóns in the D'Arienzo orchestra shouldn't lead us to think that the violins have just a secondary role. The opening of "**9 de julio**" has wonderfully sharp staccato playing from the violins which continues virtually throughout the entire track. It's something you can hear on many D'Arienzo recordings.

For the solo, D'Arienzo has a *guardia vieja* trick up his sleeve: the first violin playing a very simple solo low on the fourth string. From 1940 onwards this was the violin of Cayetano Puglisi. For some it is sad that a musician of such calibre was reduced to playing such simple phrases, but I like to think that Puglisi was pleased to give so much joy to millions of people when his own attempt to form an orchestra had not met with commercial success.

The piano

The axis of any orchestra, the sound of D'Arienzo's piano was defined by Biagi: punctuating phrases rather than linking them.

The singer

The D'Arienzo sound was organised around the rhythm and not the melody. This had consequences for the singer. The role offered to him was quite definitely that of the *estribillista* – a singer of refrains – and not that of *cantor de orquesta* – orchestra singer, although D'Arienzo would get pulled in this direction in the early 1940s. This was proudly proclaimed on the discs themselves, where you will read: "Estribillo cantado por…" – refrain sung by…

The best fit, without a doubt, was Alberto Echagüe. A *porteño* (native of Buenos Aires) might refer to his tough style as *canyengue* – an untranslatable word, but here meaning something like street-wise. He was perfect for D'Arienzo, who would struggle to replace him when he lost him in March 1940 – but that's another story.

The melody

Whilst D'Arienzo doesn't focus on the melody (the tune), of course it's still there – but instead of a smooth melody, he chops it into a series of discrete steps, like cutting a staircase into the side of a mountain. The supreme example would be his killer version of the milonga "**Silueta porteña**". Biagi's piano bubbles along underneath – it's irresistible.

What to listen to

From the band's inception in 1935 until the end of 1939 (when D'Arienzo lost every member of his orchestra including singer Alberto Echagüe – more about this later) D'Arienzo recorded 116 numbers with not a single poor track among them. I've listed them at the end of the chapter. You should listen to *all of them!* They really are that good. Unbelievably, and perhaps displaying some of the prejudice against D'Arienzo that still exists in Argentina, these have never been reprinted in their entirety outside Japan, so we'll just have to make do with what we can find: the first two CDs in RCA Victor's 15 disc 'Homenaje en RCA Victor', and Sus primeros éxitos on 'Tango Argentino' (there are two volumes, of which the first is the best). The tracks with Echagüe are particularly hard to find: only Magenta has a CD and it goes in and out of print.

There are three pianists in this period: Lidio Fasoli (10 sides), Rodolfo Biagi (66 sides) and Juan Polito (40 sides). If Biagi is the most important of this trio, the work of the other two should not be overlooked. They are good!

The first thing that should strike you about this discography is the very high proportion of milongas and especially valses. Waltz was the dance sensation that swept the world in the late 19th Century, just as tango was to do two decades later; it was guaranteed to pull the public onto the dance floor. Such a large number of valses are a sign of the band's populist leanings.

The next thing to notice is just how prolific the orchestra is. In 1937 they are in the studio no less than thirteen times, recording a couple of numbers on each occasion; in 1938, fourteen times. No wonder: in financial terms this was the most successful orchestra.

This success meant that D'Arienzo could re-record and re-issue his most popular numbers every time the sound of the band evolved. He recorded quite a few tangos three or four times; in the case of "La cumparsita", it was seven times. Consequently one can't assume, just because a track is on this list, that the recording date is the one below. It could be decades later. We'll talk about the subsequent phases of the orchestra this later on in the book. You'll soon get to hear the difference.

The fidelity of the transfers is variable. No masters survive, and all the transfers are made either from 78s or from later LP compilations. Sometimes you will hear some "reverb" (reverberation): in this case, you can be fairly sure that you are listening to an LP transfer. Adding reverb disguises some of the imperfections in the source material and back in the 1970s it was a common trick. However, even in 2005, Sony-BMG used a little reverberation in their 15 disc series 'Homenaje en RCA Victor'. For many years the best transfers have come from Japan, where dedicated collectors take great care to preserve the fidelity of the source material[2].

---

[2] We explain more about this in chapter 28.

D'Arienzo's early hits on CD/mp3

	label	no.	Album	year
CD	TARG	63341	Sus primeros éxitos vol.1 [3]	1998
CD	Magenta	9101	La Morocha canta: Alberto Echagüe [4]	2002
CD	BMG	669330	De pura cepa (1935-1936)	2005
CD	BMG	669331	El esquinazo (1937-1938)	2005
CD	BMG	669333	Meta fierro – Yunta brava (1939-1940)	2005
mp3	Magenta		Juan D'Arienzo (1937-1938)	2010

One might guess that the Magenta mp3 album 'Juan D'Arienzo (1937-1938)' is just a digital release of material from its earlier CDs, but it isn't. It has some really clean transfers with no reverberation. I wonder where they got them from.

For those with long arms and deep pockets, there are some great collections from Japan. Starting around 1998, Club Tango Argentino published the complete works of D'Arienzo on CD. This was the best D'Arienzo series in the world, but most of these albums are now sadly out-of-print. However in 2010 a new label called Audio Park printed an 11 CD compilation called 'Epoca de oro' (APCD-65xx). Volume 2 (APCD-6502) is essential for the serious DJ or collector.

[3] "primeros éxitos" means "first hits". Many albums on this label ('Tango Argentino', the tango imprint of BMG Argentina) have this title.

[4] Here the album is named after the tango "La morocha". Argentine CDs often have the name of a tango in the title of the album. Mostly they don't place them in quotation marks, because you are expected to know that this is a famous tango.

Juan D'Arienzo: discography 1935-1939

Piano: Lidio Fasoli

1	02.07.35	Desde el alma		vals
2	02.07.35	Hotel Victoria		
3	12.08.35	Penas de amor		vals
4	12.08.35	Tinta verde		
5	03.10.35	Re, fa, si		
6	03.10.35	Francia		vals
7	18.11.35	De pura cepa		milonga
8	18.11.35	Sábado inglés		
9	12.12.35	Joaquina		
10	12.12.35	Pabellón de las rosas		vals

Piano: Rodolfo Biagi

11	31.12.35	Orillas de plata		vals
12	31.12.35	9 de julio		
13	14.01.36	La guitarrita		
14	14.01.36	Silueta porteña	Walter Cabral	milonga
15	31.01.36	Retintín		
16	31.01.36	Sueño florido		vals
17	03.04.36	Un placer	Walter Cabral	vals
18	03.04.36	El flete		
19	08.05.36	Tu olvido	Walter Cabral	vals
20	08.05.36	Lorenzo		
21	09.06.36	Irene	Walter Cabral	vals
22	09.06.36	La payanca		
23	03.07.36	Don Esteban		
23/1	03.07.36	Don Esteban		
24	03.07.36	No llores madre		vals
25	05.08.36	El irresistible		
26	05.08.36	Inolvidable		vals
27	03.09.36	Rawson		
28	03.09.36	Amor y celos		vals
29	29.09.36	Don Juan		
30	29.09.36	Lágrimas y sonrisas		vals
31	27.10.36	Comme il faut		
32	27.10.36	Una lágrima		vals
33	27.11.36	Ataniche		
34	27.11.36	Corazón de artista		vals
35	30.12.36	La viruta		

36	30.12.36	Visión celeste		vals
37	21.01.37	Fachiamo la polquita		polca
38	21.01.37	El baqueano		
39	05.03.37	Qué noche!		
40	05.03.37	Alma dolorida		vals
41	01.04.37	El apronte		
42	01.04.37	Mentías		vals
43	27.04.37	Homero		
44	27.04.37	La puñalada		milonga
45	02.06.37	Amelia		polca
46	02.06.37	El cachafaz		
47	02.07.37	La rosarina		
48	02.07.37	Pasión		vals
49	26.07.37	El choclo		
50	26.07.37	Valsecito criollo		vals
51	31.08.37	Valsecito de antes		vals
52	31.08.37	El porteñito		
53	22.09.37	El caburé		
54	22.09.37	Milonga vieja milonga		milonga
55	29.10.37	Paciencia	Enrique Carbel	
56	29.10.37	Jueves		
57	09.12.37	Gallo ciego		
58	09.12.37	El cencerro		
59	14.12.37	La cumparsita		
60	14.12.37	El africano		
61	21.12.37	La morocha		
62	21.12.37	Melodía porteña		
63	04.01.38	El esquinazo		milonga
64	04.01.38	Indiferencia	Alberto Echagüe	
65	07.01.38	Rodríguez Peña		
66	07.01.38	Unión Cívica		
67	23.03.38	La mariposa		
68	23.03.38	El triunfo		
69	12.04.38	El horizonte		
70	12.04.38	El aeroplano		vals
71	06.05.38	Milonga del corazón	Alberto Echagüe	milonga
72	06.05.38	El cisne		
73	08.06.38	La catrera		
74	08.06.38	El temblor	Alberto Echagüe	milonga
75	22.06.38	Champagne tango		
76	22.06.38	Pensalo bien	Alberto Echagüe	

The slash number (23/1) indicates an alternate take. There were almost certainly many more, but this is the only one we know of that was issued.

Piano: Juan Polito

77	08.07.38	El internado		
78	08.07.38	Nada más	Alberto Echagüe	
79	05.08.38	Florida		
80	05.08.38	Estampa de varón	Alberto Echagüe	milonga
81	26.08.38	Lelia		
82	26.08.38	La bruja	Alberto Echagüe	
83	30.09.38	En tu corazón	Alberto Echagüe	vals
84	30.09.38	Lunes		
85	03.11.38	De mi flor		
86	03.11.38	Cabeza de novia	Alberto Echagüe	vals
87	09.11.38	Milonga querida	Alberto Echagüe	milonga
88	09.11.38	Ansiedad	Alberto Echagüe	
89	28.12.38	No mientas	Alberto Echagüe	
90	28.12.38	El pollito		
91	04.01.39	Pico blanco		
92	04.01.39	Yunta brava		
93	03.03.39	Meta fierro	Alberto Echagüe	milonga
94	03.03.39	Dos guitas	Alberto Echagüe	
95	18.04.39	Maipo		
96	18.04.39	No me lo digas		
97	04.05.39	El Marne		
98	04.05.39	Recuerdos de la pampa	Alberto Echagüe	vals
99	30.05.39	Charamusca		
100	30.05.39	Olvídame	Alberto Echagüe	
101	17.07.39	Derecho viejo		
102	17.07.39	Milonga del recuerdo	Alberto Echagüe	milonga
103	09.08.39	Mandria	Alberto Echagüe	
104	09.08.39	Castigo	Alberto Echagüe	vals
105	01.09.39	Felicia		
106	01.09.39	El vino triste	Alberto Echagüe	
107	27.09.39	De antaño	Alberto Echagüe	milonga
108	27.09.39	Santa milonguita	Alberto Echagüe	
109	27.09.39	Don Pacifico		
110	27.09.39	Qué importa!	Alberto Echagüe	
111	31.10.39	La cicatríz	Alberto Echagüe	milonga
112	31.10.39	Pampa		
113	14.11.39	Qué Dios te ayude	Alberto Echagüe	
114	14.11.39	Ay Aurora	Alberto Echagüe	vals
115	22.12.39	Por qué razón?		
116	22.12.39	Trago amargo	Alberto Echagüe	

2/ Aníbal Troilo &

the rise of the orchestra singer

Listening guide

ORQUESTA ANÍBAL TROILO

1/ Toda mi vida (1941)
(canta: Francisco Fiorentino)

2/ Milongueando en el '40 (1941)

3/ C.T.V. (1942)

4/ Comme il faut (1938)

The orchestra that stands most in opposition to that of Juan D'Arienzo is that of Aníbal Troilo. Not because Troilo loved the melody more than D'Arienzo – everyone did! What Troilo did more than anyone else – what he enabled the others to do – was to give the melody to the singer, not as a soloist carrying a song, but as an instrument within the orchestra, its most expressive instrument.

Back in the 1930s there were many famous tango soloists. The most famous was Carlos Gardel, one of the greatest singers, not just of tango music in the early 20th Century but of any music at any time. Gardel however never sang for dancers. All but a tiny number of his recordings were made with the backing of guitars. His aim was to convey the lyric, something he did supremely well; but no-one thought that this was possible with a dance orchestra. They played instrumental numbers; or if there was a singer, he sang just a part of the lyric. This is exactly the formula which D'Arienzo followed when he began.

But there were those who began to think differently. Dancing, or lyrics? Let's do both!

The man who made this idea a reality was Aníbal Troilo. He forged a new relationship between the orchestra and its vocalist who was now no longer an *estribillista* – a singer of vocal refrains – but the *cantor de orquesta* – the orchestra singer. This set the stage for the peak of the Golden Age, the glorious decade of the 1940s.

Now we are not saying that Troilo was the first to have a singer in the orchestra. From 1935 - 1938, Canaro has Roberto Maida whilst Fresedo has Roberto Ray right through the 1930s. Aren't they orchestra singers as well?

Well, no they are not, at least not until the end of 1938. It's time to listen to some music and at the same time learn the structure of a vocal tango of the 1940s. It's often said that a classic tango lasts three minutes. That's made up of five or six chunks of 30~40 seconds (8 bars of music) each. In a sung tango, this normally means a verse (A) and a chorus (B), like this:

1	0'00" – 0'30"	verse	instrumental
2	0'30" – 1'00"	chorus	instrumental
3	1'00" – 1'30"	1st verse	Fiorentino
4	1'30" – 2'00"	chorus	Fiorentino
(5)	2'00" – 2'30"	2nd verse	solo
(6)	2'30" – 3'00"	chorus	mystery!

plan of a Troilo-Fiorentino tango
the number of sections is not fixed, but the first four are always the same

Now if you are a dancer this is fantastic news. What this means is that there is a map to guide you through every vocal tango. The first four sections are the same every time. The band first introduces the music with an instrumental verse and a chorus. After one minute or so the singer makes his entrance and sings a verse and a chorus. This is the novelty: the *estribillista* of the early 30s wouldn't be singing the verse at this point (we call this the first verse because it's the first verse of the lyrics in the sheet music). He would wait for the next chorus (section 4 in our table) – hence the name (*estribillista* means a singer of the refrain or chorus). The change, for both Canaro and Fresedo, comes in November 1938. For Canaro, the first song with the new pattern is "Callecita de mi novia"; for Fresedo, it's "Dulce amargura".

So, we've had an instrumental verse and chorus, and now a sung verse and chorus. At this point, we don't know whether there are going to be five or six sections. We don't know whether the band is going to play the second verse or cut straight to the final chorus, and we don't know whether the singer will come back; but we do know a couple of things. First of all, we know that the second verse is never sung. That's right! *The second verse is never sung.* From this it follows that if the singer does comes back, it's the final chorus so it must be the end. This final burst of the singer takes the place of the *variación* as the climax of the piece. Listen to any of the classic 1941 sides with Fiorentino on vocals and you'll find that they conform to this pattern.

Let's begin with "**Toda mi vida**" for which Troilo himself wrote the music. You'll hear Fiorentino make his entrance after a minute, and when he does so the melody he sings is the same melody that the orchestra introduced earlier. Fiorentino is the emblematic orchestra singer. In a field of great quality, he is to this day considered the best orchestra singer of all time. Although he would eventually leave Troilo to go solo he is so identified with Troilo that it's customary to utter their names in the same breath, like this: Troilo-Fiorentino. It's the same with all the great partnerships of the 1940s, such as Pugliese-Chanel, Tanturi-Castillo, Di Sarli-Rufino, and many others.

The Troilo sound

The Troilo sound, often described as "brilliant" (in the sense of shining) is characterised by rich arrangements which alternate quite rapidly between staccato (choppy) and legato (smooth) passages. Tango may have begun in the street, but the quality of the musicianship is very high – the equal of a symphony orchestra.

The piano

Once again, the key man in the Troilo orchestra is the pianist – **Orlando Goñi**. He developed a whole new style of tango piano playing that became known as *marcación bordoneada.* Marcación means to keep *la marca* i.e. to keep time, whilst *bordoneada* refers to the base notes. *Marcación bordoneada* means that the base line is decorated without losing the beat, and the Goñi style is marvellously fluid and elastic. Listen to the instrumental "**C.T.V.**" for a tour-de-force of his playing!

In terms of importance, Goñi is to Troilo as Biagi is to D'Arienzo, only more so. Goñi was so good that he never played from arrangements. His spontaneous improvisations were always better than anything an arranger could come up with. It was marvellous for Troilo to have such an outstanding talent in his band, but it meant that he was truly irreplaceable. His replacements had to try and copy his style, as Biagi's had done, but it was an impossible task. When he leaves the orchestra in September 1943 the drop in quality is dramatic. Whilst Goñi's departure is a huge loss for us, for him it was tragic: Goñi had no head for the business aspects of running an orchestra and drank himself to death within two years. There has never been a pianist to equal him since.

The violins

The violins aren't heavily featured in Troilo's orchestra. If they get a solo, it's just a short one. Nevertheless, the quality of the musicianship is very high. Just listen to their tone in the opening of "**Pájaro ciego**" or the violin duet in "**Guapeando**".

The bandoneón

Troilo is hailed as the best bandoneón player ever in terms of feeling. And yet, even after all this effusion about the musical qualities of the orchestra, the bandoneóns are less prominent than one might think. Troilo's solos are modest and restrained – much the same thing that one might say about the piano playing of Don Osvaldo Pugliese.

Milongueando en el '40

"**Milongueando en el '40**" is the title of an instrumental track that formed a key part of the repertoire of the orchestra. Don't be confused by the title: it does not mean dancing milonga, but has the same root as the word ***milonguero***. Now, a ***milonguero*** is someone who takes their cultural identity from being at the milonga. "Milongueando en el '40" therefore means something like "Milonga life in 1940". The opening phrase is a fantastic tumbling syncopation – let's count it through:

count:	**1** 2 3	**1** 2 3	**1** 2 3	**1** 2 3	**1** 2	**1** 2	**1**
grouping:	3	3	3	3	2	2	1

Milongueando en el '40: we've got syncopation!

It's very exciting and certainly much more complex than what the public were used to hearing. With this piece, Troilo is saying: it's 1940 and the new wave is here – the old guard can move over!

Now, some of you will have noticed that Milongueando en el '40 is recorded not in 1940 but in 1941. What was happening with the Troilo band in 1940? When, in fact, did the band start?

The answer is a little frustrating: the Troilo orchestra formed in 1937, emerging from the nucleus of Juan Carlos Cobián's orchestra. Disbanding after the carnival season (the end of summer, i.e. March or so), Troilo took with him musicians with whom he'd been playing for several years, including Orlando Goñi. The band made their first recordings for the Odeón label in March 1938 and then – nothing.

When you start looking at discographies, an interesting fact emerges: Odeón, after a glorious history in the 20s, developed a nasty habit in the late 30s of signing up new talent not in order to promote them, but simply to prevent them from signing to the competition, which was Victor. Those first two recordings – both instrumentals – are with Odeón: the rest are with Victor. They did the same to Tanturi. Three years of unrecorded material… nevertheless, the 1938 sides are available (although not on any CDs produced by Sony-BMG, who own RCA Victor). They make fascinating listening, particularly the 1938 recording of "**Comme il faut**". We are lucky to have this recording because it doesn't really belong to the repertoire of a sophisticated orchestra like Troilo's which is in the vanguard of the evolution of tango. Different orchestras chose different repertoire according to their level of sophistication and whether or not they were focussed on the lyrics. "**Comme il faut**" is a *guardia vieja* composition, much more typical of say the D'Arienzo orchestra with which we can compare it.

The D'Arienzo recording was made a year and a half earlier (October 1936) so it's not a straight comparison: tango music was evolving fast at this time and we can posit that by March 1938 D'Arienzo would be playing harder and faster. Even allowing for this, playing these two versions side by side is shocking. The Troilo version is like a whirlwind, reminiscent of Láurenz and the mythical Vardaro-Pugliese sextet (which we'll talk about in Chapter 11). It just blows the D'Arienzo version out of the water. Not only is it brighter and more sophisticated, it is more vigorous and more varied rhythmically: Troilo imposes a 3-3-2 syncopation on the melody that had never been there before. D'Arienzo is king of the beat, but he's not always the king of rhythm.

Troilo on CD

Unlike D'Arienzo, the more sophisticated music of Troilo has been kept in print for a very long time. RCA Victor, with whom Troilo was signed throughout the 1940s and again in the 1960s, reprinted all his output with them over 26 LPs back in the 1970s. The masters prepared at this time, warts and all, have formed the basis for all subsequent CD issues.

BMG produced some Troilo CDs on their 'Tango Argentino' label in 1996 themed by singer. Then in 1997 they issued the magnificent 16 CD series 'Obra Completa en RCA'. This series was carefully prepared for the serious listener or collector, with all recording dates, matrix and disc numbers[5], and extensive sleeve notes. This series was deleted but then in 2005 BMG produced a new series, 'Troilo en RCA Victor' – 26 CDs, one for each LP. These are multimedia CDs with some nice bonus goodies but they are not such good value for money. Neither series has the two tracks recorded in 1938 because, being recorded on Odeón, EMI have the rights and not BMG.

Early Troilo on CD: what to listen to

We begin with the first two CDs in BMG's 'Troilo en RCA Victor'.

BMG	659436	Yo Soy el Tango (1941)	2005
BMG	659437	Tinta Roja (1941/1942)	2005

[5] the matrix is the name given to the physical master made during the recording

Troilo – Goñi discography

Here's the Troilo – Goñi discography. Have a look: what do you notice?

Compared to the D'Arienzo discography there are far fewer milongas and valses. This is a proper tango orchestra if you please!

We've excluded the acetates made from live radio recordings. Although they are interesting to listen to and give extra insight into the band, the fidelity is poor and they are in any case difficult to obtain.

1	07.03.38	Comme il faut		
2	07.03.38	Tinta verde		
3	04.03.41	Yo soy el tango	Fiorentino	
4	04.03.41	Mano brava	Fiorentino	milonga
5	04.03.41	Toda mi vida	Fiorentino	
6	04.03.41	Cachirulo		
7	16.04.41	Con toda la voz que tengo	Fiorentino	milonga
8	16.04.41	Te aconsejo que me olvides	Fiorentino	
9	28.05.41	Tabernero	Fiorentino	
10	28.05.41	Pájaro ciego	Fiorentino - Mandarino	
11	17.06.41	El bulín de la calle Ayacucho	Fiorentino	
12	17.06.41	Milongueando en el '40		
13	11.07.41	Guapeando		
14	11.07.41	Una carta	Fiorentino	
15	18.07.41	En esta tarde gris	Fiorentino	
16	18.07.41	Cordón de oro		
17	08.09.41	Total, pa' que sirvo	Fiorentino	
18	08.09.41	El cuarteador	Fiorentino	
19	09.10.41	Maragata	Fiorentino	
20	09.10.41	Tu diagnóstico	Fiorentino	vals
21	09.10.41	Cautivo	Fiorentino	
22	23.10.41	Tinta roja	Fiorentino	
23	23.10.41	No le digas que la quiero	Fiorentino	
24	23.10.41	El tamango		
25	21.11.41	Sencillo y compadre	Fiorentino	
26	21.11.41	Del tiempo guapo	Fiorentino	milonga
27	08.01.42	Malena	Fiorentino	
27/1	08.01.42	Malena	Fiorentino	
28	08.01.42	C.T.V.		
29	16.04.42	Mi castigo	Fiorentino	
30	16.04.42	Papá Baltasar	Fiorentino	milonga

31	16.04.42	Pa' que bailen los muchachos	Fiorentino	
32	12.06.42	Fueye	Fiorentino	
33	12.06.42	Un placer		vals
34	12.06.42	Colorao, colorao	Fiorentino	
35	15.06.42	Soy un muchacho de la guardia	Fiorentino	
36	15.06.42	Suerte loca	Fiorentino	
37	15.06.42	Los mareados	Fiorentino	
38	23.07.42	Acordándome de vos	Fiorentino	vals
39	23.07.42	La tablada		
40	01.09.42	Lejos de Buenos Aires	Fiorentino	
41	01.09.42	El encopao	Fiorentino	
42	10.09.42	Pedacito de cielo	Fiorentino	vals
43	18.09.42	Tristezas de la calle Corrientes	Fiorentino	
44	18.09.42	No te apures carablanca	Fiorentino	
45	09.10.42	Ficha de oro	Fiorentino	milonga
46	09.10.42	La maleva		
47	22.10.42	El chupete		
48	22.10.42	De pura cepa		milonga
49	30.10.42	Gricel	Fiorentino	
50	14.12.42	Barrio de tango	Fiorentino	
51	14.12.42	Pa' que seguir	Fiorentino	
52	14.12.42	Por las calles de la vida	Fiorentino	
53	29.12.42	Buenos Aires	Fiorentino	
54	11.03.43	Corazón... no le hagas caso	Fiorentino	
55	11.03.43	Margarita Gauthier	Fiorentino	
56	25.03.43	Percal	Fiorentino	
57	25.03.43	Valsecito amigo	Fiorentino	vals
58	05.04.43	Tango y copas	Marino	
59	05.04.43	Cada vez que me recuerdes	Fiorentino	
60	27.04.43	Cuando tallan los recuerdos	Marino	
61	27.04.43	Soy del 90	Fiorentino	
62	03.05.43	Inspiración		
63	03.05.43	Ropa blanca	Marino	milonga
64	03.05.43	Soy un porteño	Fiorentino	milonga
65	02.06.43	De barro	Fiorentino	
66	02.06.43	Farolito de papel	Marino	
67	30.06.43	Uno	Marino	
68	04.08.43	Soñar y nada más	Fiorentino - Marino	vals
69	04.08.43	Tal vez será su voz	Marino	
70	04.08.43	Garúa	Fiorentino	
71	04.08.43	El distinguido ciudadano		
72	30.09.43	Cantando se van las penas	Marino	
73	30.09.43	Farol	Fiorentino	

3 / Osvaldo Pugliese:

passion, integrity, and a red carnation

He broke through the abyss which exists between the head and the heart

- Alejandro Prevignano

Listening guide

ORQUESTA
OSVALDO PUGLIESE

1/ Recuerdo (1944)

2/ Tierra querida (1944)

3/ La yumba (1946)

4/ Negracha (1948)

5/ Malandraca (1949)

6/ Muchachos comienza la ronda (1943)
canta: Roberto Chanel

Osvaldo Pugliese was the last of our Big Four to achieve stardom. Born in 1905, he made his first recording only in 1943, with an orchestra he had put together in 1939. The music of Osvaldo Pugliese is the most passionate in tango. This is something that everyone who hears it understands intuitively, even if they find it hard to dance to, but not only is it the most passionate: it is the most pure. So, start listening to "**La yumba**" – the earlier, 1946 recording – and then carry on reading.

Pugliese was a man of great integrity. A lifetime communist, he ran his band as a collective, with everyone receiving an equal share. In the 1950s he spent several years in jail for his beliefs, writing the arrangements in his cell. His musicians were devoted to him: the core line-up of his band was unchanged from its inception in 1939 until 1968. When he was in jail a red carnation would be placed on the keyboard of the piano in his honour.

Pugliese's music is definitely urban with a unique and characteristic driving *marcato*. Identifying himself with the inheritance of Julio De Caro and the 4 x 4, he took De Caro's music and clothed it in humanity.

La yumba

Pugliese described his sound as ***yumba*** (pronounced "zhoom-ba"): a strong attack of the whole orchestra, led by the piano and double bass, on beats 1 and 3 ("zhoom"), with rumbling bass octaves in the piano on beats 2 and 4 ("ba"), like this; ONE two THREE four. This is an urban music, reflecting the brutal and mechanical impulses of both the city and the factory. Pugliese once said that one of his inspirations was the sound of metalworkers. We can hear them, and also the working man walking the busy city streets.

The Pugliese sound: hard-soft

The Pugliese beat has an unrelenting drive that is reflected in the entire orchestra. It is a veritable musical machine, like an old fashioned car engine in which the pistons are the bandoneóns.

Even the violins play with a hard attacking sound, ratcheting up the tension. Just when you can't stand it anymore, the music softens and melts, allowing you to draw breath. But this respite is only temporary: very soon, the engine starts up again, the yum-ba *marcato* driving you on towards the climax.

This hard-soft contrast is much stronger than the staccato-legato contrast of Troilo; we can say it's extreme. In the soft passages, the *compás* itself disappears, flummoxing the beginning dancer completely. In the hard passages, the music does not ask, it demands. Surely this is the music that the dancer Juan Carlos Copes had in mind when he declared of tango: "The music arouses and torments, the dance is the coupling of a man and a woman defenceless against the world and powerless to change things".

As with Julio De Caro, this is an orchestra where you can name every member; not just in the piano of Don Osvaldo himself, but in all the instruments. The first bandoneón can only be **Osvaldo Ruggiero**, the composer of the 1947 hit "**N.N.**". His are the fingers which make *variaciones* such as those in "**Recuerdo**" sound effortless.

The first violin is **Enrique Camerano**, born it was said to play with Pugliese, although it's impossible to ignore the contribution of **Julio Carrasco** and (from 1943 onwards) **Oscar Herrero**. How about that: this is an orchestra in which the names of the second violins are remembered. The double bass meanwhile is **Alcides Rossi**, whom Pugliese considered so important to his orchestra that he gave him the first ever double-bass solo in tango in their 1947 recording of "**Jueves**". These men stayed with Pugliese from 1939 until October 1968 – almost thirty years.

Through to the end of his life, Don Osvaldo, with characteristic humility, named Francisco De Caro as the inspiration for his own playing and said that his aim was only to rescue the inheritance of De Caro, which he felt was in danger of becoming lost. This is to completely understate the contribution of the Pugliese orchestra.

To show his band what he wanted he wrote his famous tango "**La yumba**", the first of a trio of instrumentals that define his work. The other two are "**Negracha**" and "**Malandraca**". It has been suggested that the word *yumba* is African[6], like the words *tango* and *milonga*, although Pugliese himself said that he made the word up.

"**La yumba**" appeared in 1946, "**Negracha**" in 1948 and "**Malandraca**" in 1949. The story goes that Pugliese started work on them many years earlier, only publishing them once he felt they were mature. If "**La yumba**" is Pugliese's anthem, then "**Negracha**" is his manifesto. Years before the phrase "avant-garde" was first used in tango Pugliese had anticipated it in a work where history and the future collide. Today it still sounds not just modern but daring, and remains the benchmark against which any modern work must be judged; not least because it does what it does without leaving tango. Compared to those who came later, this is an achievement which remains without equal.

Negracha

When Pugliese was playing at the Piccadilly club, the black girls there asked him for music with more rhythm. His answer was "**Negracha**".

There had been syncopation in tango music before: Canaro uses it as far back as 1929, Pracánico even earlier. But never before had there been syncopation like this – and there probably never will be again. All those who say that Piazzolla introduced syncopation into tango music should listen to "**Negracha**" (and to Canaro) before coming out with their pronouncements.

---

[6] Robert Farris Thompson, "Tango: An Art History of Love" (Hardcover) New York, Pantheon Books 2005 pp200-202

In an article analysing the structure of the piece[7], the bandoneón player Rodolfo Mederos was lavish in his praise for the work and its author, seeing in it the joining of past and future.

> *There are those who hear the music only after it's played: they are the majority. Then there are those who hear it when it plays: they are few. Finally, there are those who hear it before it's played. Osvaldo Pugliese perceived what had previously not existed and composed "Negracha"*
>
> *Negracha is more than music, it is music for those to come.*
>
> *Arnold Schoenberg said that there exist in man two opposing tendencies which are always in struggle. One wishes to reproduce pleasurable stimuli (the known, that is to say, experiences already lived, calming if you will), and the other which wishes to produce new sensations, which are at first disconcerting. Perhaps this last is what has happened with Negracha.*
>
> *Negracha leaves cheap and warm melancholy to one side… Negracha is a unique and definitive work. It is a flame which breathes and warms. It is for those who will come afterwards.*
>
> – Rodolfo Mederos

Pugliese's music is dramatic but it is not something showy or external. Rather, it is something that arises from within, demanding expression. It is not music that can be listened to in the background, but *demands* your full involvement – your full attention and participation. I can barely imagine what it must have been like to dance to his orchestra for a whole evening. A single tanda of three numbers leaves me wrung out like a wet flannel.

[7] "Negracha: Los que oyen antes de que suene (Those who hear before it sounds)" Rodolfo Mederos, Buenos Aires Tango y lo demás – diciembre 1991

Pugliese: just an instrumental band?

The discussion we have just had confined itself to the instrumentals, the clearest way to appreciate the Pugliese style. This could easily lead one to believe that the Pugliese orchestra is just an instrumental band – an impression that would also be easy to acquire from the selection of his music that is played in most milongas. Is it true?

Well, Pugliese's singers in the 1950s and 1960s were pretty dire from the dancer's point of view – but so were D'Arienzo's, and even Troilo's best period for the vocal numbers is the 1940s. For Pugliese it's the same. When he first started recording in 1943 he had a fantastic singer, **Roberto Chanel**, and the combination Pugliese-Chanel was as famous as the other leading partnerships of the day, such as Troilo-Fiorentino or D'Arienzo-Echagüe. To give you an idea, listen to "**Muchachos comienza la ronda**" which is from their second recording session together. Chanel has a powerful voice with a nasal tone – a bit like Echagüe but with much more class. The choice of repertoire must also be remarked upon: the title means, "The lads are forming the circle", and the lyric adds, "… which the tango invites you to form". It's a lyric that deals amongst other things with the social aspect of dancing tango, how it is a group activity that takes place in community. That's something we would do well to remember.

Osvaldo Pugliese today

Pugliese lived until 1995 which meant he lived to see the tango revival – the only one of the Big Four orchestra leaders to do so. For those who love him Pugliese is a living presence. His fans call him *San Pugliese*: Saint Pugliese.

Classic Pugliese on CD: what to listen to

The Pugliese style was demanding for the recording technology of the day and recordings have aged less well than many others. We have to be especially careful about the fidelity. There are plenty of CDs which aren't worth buying – and others which one might dismiss on first listening but then return to later because the fidelity really is the best available.

These first two recommendations cover Pugliese's entire oeuvre, both instrumental and vocal. They have excellent sound fidelity. There are many more good CDs available but we'll talk about them later when we return for an in-depth look at the orchestra.

EMI	855386	Ausencia	1995
EMI	335997	Edición Aniversario (4 CDs)	2005

4/ Carlos Di Sarli: doing it with strings

Listening guide

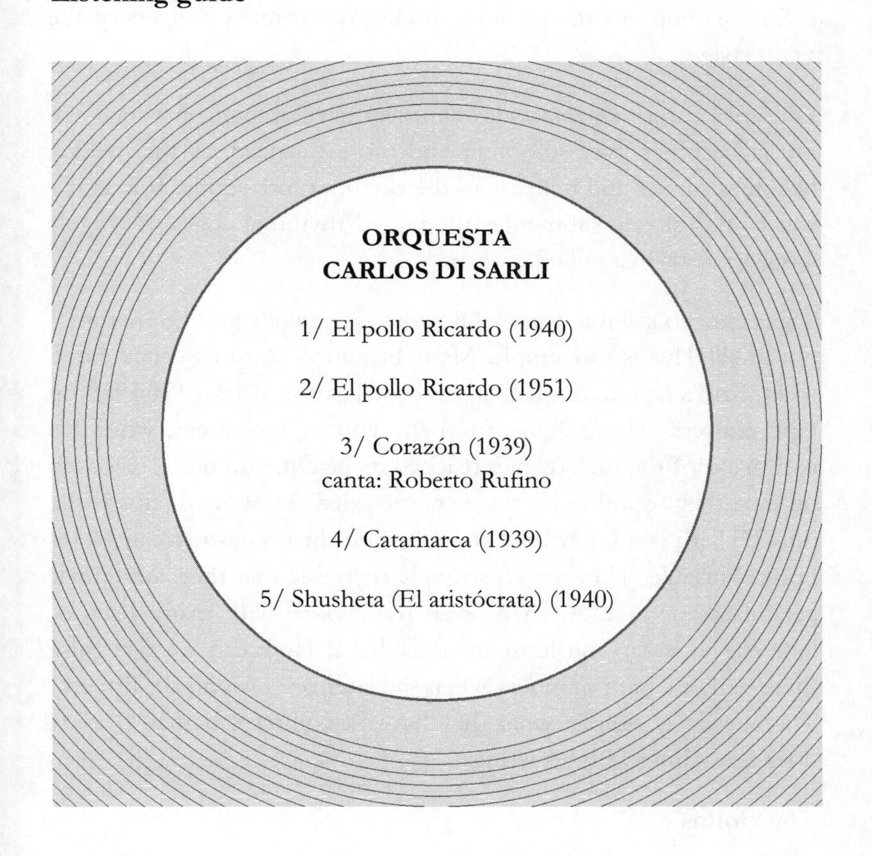

The orchestra which gave the most emphasis to the melody was that of Carlos Di Sarli. His command of the melody, combined with a steady walking beat, makes him one of the most popular orchestras for dancing right up to the present day. At the same time, the Di Sarli orchestra is not simply aiming at being a party orchestra. This is music that is elegant and classy at the same time as maintaining a great *compás* for the dancers. This is not an easy trick to pull off; no wonder it's the favourite orchestra for many dancers of the salon style.

Di Sarli's career shows a clear musical development in which the music becomes ever smoother and more nuanced, as the melody becomes slower and richer, and the rhythm more subtle. It is as if a watery tide slowly submerges the jagged rhythmic edges of tango's staccato beats in a melodic wash.

This is not to say that Carlos Di Sarli is all melody and no rhythm – not at all! This is too simple. Many beginners learn to dance tango to Di Sarli's late instrumentals, recorded in the years 1954-1958 on tape masters. These come from the end of his career, when his command of the melody had reached its height, and being recorded on tape they sound as if they were recorded yesterday. If this is the only Di Sarli you know then you may find the orchestra's early sides unrecognisable. They are so strongly rhythmic that they sometimes get mistaken for D'Arienzo, even by *tangueros* with many years of listening to tango music under their belts. How can we recognise these early Di Sarli numbers when the later ones sound so different? The answer is simple: what they have in common is that Di Sarli does everything with his strings.

The violins

The constant of Di Sarli's career is not so much the melody as the *violins*. He uses them for everything: not just for melody, but for rhythm as well, and this is the foolproof way to identify his recordings. Whilst D'Arienzo's orchestra is driven by the bandoneóns, Di Sarli's is led – or rather, appears to be led – by the violins. For his rhythm, Di Sarli makes the violins play staccato, and the bandoneóns fill in: you almost can't hear them. A classic example would be the 1940 recording of "**El pollo Ricardo**" (again, be careful: the band recorded this three times and this version is not the one most often played). The opening staccato phrases are all in the violins, supported by bandoneóns. And when the *variación* comes at the end, the violin gets that as well!

Di Sarli uses the same techniques on all the band's early instrumentals. In the band's next recording, "**Shusheta (El aristocrata)**", the variation in colour produced by the violins is even more extreme. As well as melody and attacking staccato passages we have some pizzicato in the very opening phrase; and when the bandoneóns are handed the melody shortly afterwards, the violins maintain their choppy *marcato* in the background – the opposite of what many other orchestras would do.

The piano

Just as with D'Arienzo, the piano was a key element in the Di Sarli sound. In this case it is Carlos Di Sarli himself who leads the orchestra from the piano. He is immediately identifiable from the bell-like trills in the right hand which don't punctuate the phrases, as Biagi's do, but bridge them. Di Sarli is a great musician, playing with restraint in the service of his own musical vision. As the music develops, he plays fewer and fewer notes. Only in some of his milongas does he let rip and show just what he is really capable of as a virtuoso pianist.

So, violins at the forefront: it's Di Sarli. Still not sure? The next two check points are: bell-like fills in the right hand of the piano; bandoneóns almost inaudible. Yes? It's Di Sarli.

The singer

Di Sarli had great singers throughout his career. **Roberto Rufino**, the first singer with Di Sarli's orchestra, sings their first tango  "**Corazón**" as though he knows everything about love, but he was only 17 when this was recorded and too young to gain admission to the cabarets where the orchestra played. They had to sneak him in through the back door. Rufino was joined by Alberto Podestá in 1942, but Podestá got bored with playing second fiddle to Rufino and quit after a year, returning after Rufino's departure in 1944. After Podestá comes the dark baritone of Jorge Durán (1945-47). All of them are outstanding vocalists and just great for dancing. In fact there isn't a period in Di Sarli's long career in which the quality of the music drops from the point of view of the dancer. You can dance with great pleasure to recordings from any part of his career, from the first sides with Rufino in 1939 right up to the final album in 1958, almost twenty years later. Over this period only Pugliese is as consistent. Both men were uncompromising, but Di Sarli was also a difficult personality and his inflexibility would lead him into difficulties, both with his musicians and with others in the music business.

The Di Sarli story

Born in 1903 in Bahía Blanca, Di Sarli was performing publicly at the age of 13 – the same age at which an accident with his father's gun damaged one eye, leading him to wear dark glasses for the rest of his life.

After a brief spell as one of Fresedo's pianists he formed his sextet at the end of 1927, recording from 1928-1931 at which time they lost their contract in the talking pictures revolution. (We'll talk about the era of the sextets later on).

After some years outside the capital Di Sarli put together his own orchestra at the end of 1938 and they began performing the following January. When they cut their first sides at the end of the year, the music is already fully developed.

The development of the orchestra over the years is an extraordinary one because Di Sarli moves forward without ever sacrificing dance appeal. The melody rises, submerging the rhythm in a great wash of sound, but without losing sight of the *compás*. We'll cover this in a later chapter, but to hear where he is going, try listening to the 1951 version of "**El pollo Ricardo**". From the opening notes it's clear that the pace is much slower than that of the 1940 recording, but please listen all the way through to feel the very different effect this has on your body, despite the similarity of the arrangement.

Di Sarli's touch on the piano is just amazing. He never wrote down his piano parts. He didn't need to, but he also wanted to make it difficult for people to copy his style. I've heard that sometimes he would play with the piano turned in such a way that the public couldn't see his fingerings. When he died in 1960, Troilo said of him: "El ciego se llevó el secreto a la tumba": he took his secret to the grave.

Early Di Sarli on CD: what to listen to

Well, this is embarrassing. One's introduction to Di Sarli's music normally comes with the late instrumentals, which we'll come to later, but for the early recordings there isn't a single CD which covers the ground. The best selection, and with excellent transfers, is the Euro Records album 'Milongueando en el '40 con Di Sarli y Troilo' which has twelve tracks each from Di Sarli and Troilo. Euro also have the best album to explore this material further on their 'Colección 78 RPM' imprint.

Euro	16036	Milongueando en el '40 con Di Sarli y Troilo	1995
Euro	17016	Colección 78 RPM: Carlos Di Sarli 1940-1943	2004

The Big Four: a summary

D'Arienzo: the King of the Beat. Irresistible, foot tapping beat, but a raw deal for the singer. Contrast: none! Pianist: Rodolfo Biagi.

Troilo: best orchestra for the singers. Contrast: staccato-legato. Pianist: Orlando Goñi.

Pugliese: passionate and intense. De Caro's ideas with humanity and edge. Driving beat: *la yumba.* Contrast: hard-soft. Pianist: Don Osvaldo himself.

Di Sarli: great command of the melody, did everything with the strings. Always danceable. Pianist: Di Sarli himself.

And finally: when was the Golden Age?

Tango historians talk about a Golden Age of tango lasting forty years with its high point the Golden Decade of the 1940s, when tango reached its peak. Historically speaking this is true, but what about from our perspective?

Well, the vast majority of the music played for dancing today comes from a single decade that isn't quite the Golden Decade of the 1940s. It begins with D'Arienzo and ends in the mid 40s. After this the music becomes more sophisticated and is less consistently good for dancing.

Our Golden Decade, then, would be the years 1935-1944. This might be a bit confusing, so I'll try to make it clear which one is meant as we go along.

Part 2

Other orchestras of the Golden Decade

5/ The many ages of Francisco Canaro

Listening guide

1/De puro guapo (1935)*
2/Poema (1935)* 3/Tormenta (1939)+
4/A media luz (1926) 5/Derecho viejo (1927)
6/La morocha (1929) estribillo: Ada Falcón
7/La cumparsita (2° versión) (1929)
8/Flor de fango (1931) canta: Charlo
9/Milonga sentimental (m) (1933)
10/Con tu mirar (v) (1930) canta: Charlo
11/El jardín del amor (v) (1932) cantan: Irusta/ Fugazot
12/Ronda del querer (v) (1934) 13/ Mano a mano (1938)*
14/Charamusca (1934) 15/Si yo fuera millonario (1933)+
16/Mala suerte (1939)+
17/Salud, dinero y amor (v) (1939) canta: Amor
18/Necesito olvidar (1942) canta: Adrián

* estribillo: Roberto Maida
+ canta: Ernesto Famá

Next must come Francisco Canaro, the most prolific and in financial terms the most successful tango artist of all time. This briefest of introductions already identifies the core aspect of Canaro's career: whilst he produced some fantastic music, his life – both artistic and personal – was organised around financial rather than musical values. Born into poverty, Canaro spent his whole life concerned with money, long after success had made him rich. Always aware of the tastes of his audience, he was not afraid to change his style according to what he thought would be most popular at that moment. Whilst the Big Four orchestras each have a clear musical blueprint that defines their careers, the Canaro orchestra can shift personality rather rapidly. Of these different personalities, there are some I adore and others I really don't like.

Let's begin by looking at a Canaro that we can all love, and the one that musically so nearly gives him a place at the top: the Canaro of 1935-1938 with singer Roberto Maida. This is the period of the D'Arienzo explosion and yet, with the calm and honeyed voice of Maida, Canaro is producing music of great warmth and tenderness. An example that brings this home is "**De puro guapo**" (1935), more familiar to us from the later version of Pedro Láurenz. Canaro concentrates on the *compás* which is slow, steady and strong, but the overall effect is transformed by Maida. His voice softens the mood, and the contrast between Canaro's beat and Maida's voice adds greatly to the musical interest of the whole. When

Canaro instead matches Maida the result is serene, an effect exemplified by the immortal "**Poema**" (1935).

Now for contrast let's listen to a track from just a few years later: 1939's "**Tormenta**". The effect is quite different, and it's down to the singer, **Ernesto Famá**, who does not have Maida's softness. In fact when we look at Canaro's career as a whole, a pattern emerges: an alternation between phases when his music has a harder beat and a softer beat, with the choice of singer being key in the effect created.

Minotto, musical centre of the Canaro orchestra

Canaro's orchestra is not as closely organised around the genius of individual musicians as the Big Four. Nevertheless, there is one exception: his brilliant first bandoneón, Minotto Di Cicco – Minotto for short.

Minotto had a short stint with Canaro around 1918, returning for the years 1923-1926 when he was instrumental in defining the sound of Canaro's bandoneóns, something we can verify by listening to the recordings of Minotto's own orchestra in 1930-1931. Given full creative licence, the sound of Minotto's bandoneón section sounds remarkably similar to Canaro's.

Minotto's orchestra was one of the casualties of the events of 1931[8] and he returned to Canaro in 1932, remaining with him for the rest of his career. He is the musical centre of Canaro's orchestra. His characteristic sound is clearly heard in "**Poema**" where his bandoneón fills the gaps in the violin solo.

The many ages of Francisco Canaro

Now that we've got a grip on the Canaro sound, let's try to get an overview of his whole musical career. On the one hand, Canaro was a fantastic innovator. Here is a list of his firsts, two of which he shares with Roberto Firpo:

- 1916 - replaces the flute with the double bass of Leopoldo Thomson, thus creating, along with Roberto Firpo, the *sexteto típico* (traditional sextet).
- 1920 - starts using an arranger (Luís Riccardi, his pianist). His style is the beginning of the end of the *guardia vieja.*
- 1921 - puts together a 32 piece orchestra for the carnival dance, including cellos.
- 1924 - introduces the *estribillista* (refrain singer).

---

[8] see Chapter 17, "The era of the sextets"

- 1924 - Canaro and Firpo extend the line of bandoneóns and violins, expanding the sextet into the Orquesta Típica.
- 1927 - first to have an *estribillista* as a permanent part of his orchestra (Agustín Irusta).
- 1929 - first to use a female vocalist as *estribillista.*
- 1933 - first recording of a milonga by a dance orchestra.

This is a remarkable list of achievements but the last of them is dated 1933. That's hardly a criticism when Canaro has already done so much, but as dancers we know that the vast majority of the music that we hear in the milongas comes from our own Golden Decade of 1935-1944 – the decade made possible by the D'Arienzo revolution of 1935.

Canaro's reaction to the D'Arienzo revolution was – amazingly for a man who became known as a dedicated populist – to largely ignore it. Musically, along with Fresedo, he is moving in a different direction. Having made music in the early 30s that had as strong a beat as D'Arienzo, he had taken on Roberto Maida and was making softer, more romantic music of the highest quality. He is not untouched by events; at the end of 1938 we can hear his beat become less soft, but Maida's voice keeps everything smooth.

However it would not be true to say that Canaro ignored the renewed popularity of the *guardia vieja* altogether. Seeing that the old-time quartet that Firpo established in 1936 was successful, Canaro founded one of his own in 1937: the Quinteto Don Pancho, known from the end of 1940 onwards as the Quinteto Pirincho[9].

Through 1938 the orchestra became more up-beat, but Canaro felt the need to make more extensive changes. At the end of the year he hired Francisco Amor as a second singer, but the big change came at the beginning of 1939: Canaro rehired **Ernesto Famá**. Now

---

[9] Pirincho was Canaro's nickname. It's the name of a South American bird which has an orange crest. When Francisco Canaro was born he had a tuft of hair on his head and the midwife exclaimed: "why, he looks like a *pirincho*".

Famá was a veteran of the *guardia vieja.* He had sung with Osvaldo Fresedo as far back as 1927 and had also had a previous stint with Canaro in the years 1932-1934. Canaro is falling back on a singer he knows. Maida resigned from the orchestra immediately – effectively he is replaced by Famá with Amor as the second singer. Nowadays we'd call it constructive dismissal.

Now I am going to go out on a limb here and tell you what I really think: whilst the 1939 recordings are okay, musically this is a huge step backwards for Canaro. A performance such as "**Tormenta**" (a popular track from that year that one does hear at the milonga) has lost all its subtlety and the proof is in his treatment of the rhythm, which becomes increasingly strident. However much you enjoy Canaro's 40s output – and there's so much of it that there's still plenty to enjoy – there's no denying that he has become a populist: still very successful and with his finger kept firmly on the pulse of the public but no longer breaking new ground, his innovations now confined to novelty numbers. From this point onwards Canaro's importance wanes. His tangos from the twenties are extraordinarily innovative, his milongas from the thirties are full of excitement, but the work he developed in the forties is left behind by the artists that came after him. Name any mainstream Canaro tango from this period onwards and I can name you a stronger version from another orchestra.

Let's not forget as well that Canaro was now 24 years into his recording career. Born in 1888, he was already 51 years old at this point. It shouldn't really surprise us if his creative energy is beginning to diminish.

Our first attempt to categorise Canaro's career, then, looks like this:

1. 1915-1926: the acoustic era
2. 1926-1934: the early electrical era
3. 1934-1938: the Maida era.
4. 1939 onwards: the populist era

Of these the most neglected period, and possibly the best musically, is the second one. Let's take a closer look at it.

Canaro at the beginning of the electrical era (1926-1934)

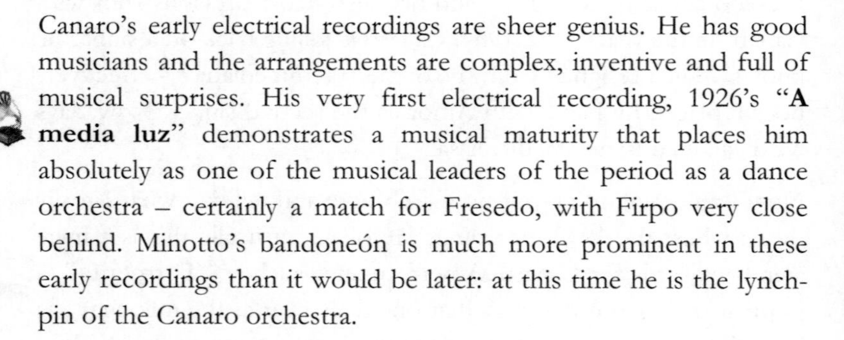

Canaro's early electrical recordings are sheer genius. He has good musicians and the arrangements are complex, inventive and full of musical surprises. His very first electrical recording, 1926's "**A media luz**" demonstrates a musical maturity that places him absolutely as one of the musical leaders of the period as a dance orchestra – certainly a match for Fresedo, with Firpo very close behind. Minotto's bandoneón is much more prominent in these early recordings than it would be later: at this time he is the lynch-pin of the Canaro orchestra.

I've marked the period until the arrival of Maida as a block, but in fact you can divide this into two. In the years 1926-1930 Canaro's recordings have the same qualities that we hear in "**A media luz**": great musicians, great arrangements, tender yet rhythmic at the same time. He also had one of the greatest voices of the day singing for him: **Charlo**. In the early 30s however Canaro's beat becomes stronger and stronger. This trend first becomes apparent in 1930 with the instrumental tango "**El púa**" and it intensifies through the next couple of years. This is the strong beat to which Canaro would return in 1939. It may just be a coincidence, but I wonder whether this has anything to do with why Charlo – a master of the tender delivery – stops recording with Canaro in 1932. His replacement? Ernesto Famá.

This division gives us the following outline of the main phases of Canaro's career:

1. 1915-1926: the acoustic era
2a. 1926-1931: the early electrical era: mostly soft. Charlo.
2b. 1932-1934: the early electrical era: mostly hard. Famá.
3. 1934-1938: the Maida era (soft)
4. 1939 onwards: the populist era: Famá, Amor, Adrián etc.

Canaro's music develops rapidly in the late 1920s. A good example would be his recording of the classic Eduardo Arolas tango

"**Derecho viejo**". Made in April 1927, only five months after "A media luz" this piece is rich with effects: pizzicato and *latigo* (*glissando* – slides) in the violins, and growling bandoneóns.

If forced to choose only one track to demonstrate the fullness and richness of his music at this early time I would have to choose his magnificent recording of "**La morocha**" from 1929, for two reasons. First of all, because of the participation of **Ada Falcón**, one of the most dramatic and expressive voices of tango. They recorded 201 numbers together but nearly all of these feature Falcón as a soloist backed by Canaro's orchestra and were not intended for dancing. There are just a handful in which she sings as an *estribillista*. This was incredibly daring, not just at the time, but right through the Golden Age of tango – even today it is extremely rare to find a woman's voice with a dance orchestra. There are good reasons for this: the tenor voice is closest in range to the violin, and so is the most easily "scored" for tango orchestra. The singer in a dance number (be they *estribillista* or *cantor de orquesta*) is not being backed by them, but behaves like an instrument within the orchestra. Canaro makes it work wonderfully, with delicate echoes of Falcón's voice in the upper register of the piano. No-one else would dare to use a woman's voice with a dance orchestra again until Donato in 1939, ten years later.

Secondly, the arrangement is just fantastic! Ada Falcón comes in just when you would expect her to, after the band has played the A + B music once through (we can't say verse and chorus because the song has only one verse). The real surprise though is the syncopated section that follows:

A	instrumental
B	instrumental
A	Ada Falcón
B	instrumental – syncopated
A	instrumental – bandoneón and violin alternating

Structure of 'La Morocha' (Canaro/Falcón, 24-07-1929)

The syncopation is amazing because it is multi-layered, with wild percussion from what sounds very much like a drum kit underneath strongly syncopated phrasing from violins and bandoneóns together. Only the piano holds it all together. The performance is a tour-de-force, and the B-side (the instrumental "**Don Juan**") is just as good. Anyone who thinks that Piazzolla introduced syncopation to tango music needs to listen to this.

When you look for "**La morocha**", be careful because Canaro would often record two versions of the same tango within the space of a few weeks, and often with the same singer: a dance version, with the singer as *estribillista*, and a *tango canción*, a song rather than a dance number, with the orchestra accompanying the singer. If you had the 78s in front of you, you could tell which was which by looking at the labels. The first would say, "Francisco Canaro. Estribillo: Ada Falcón", and the second would say, "Ada Falcón accompanied by Francisco Canaro and his orchestra". Unfortunately for us, the record companies today don't make the same distinction. They choose the order of the names according to which artist they are trying to sell.

Having savoured the emotion of Ada Falcón, we must as well listen to a tango from this period with the voice of **Charlo**, such as 1931's "**Flor de fango**". Charlo doesn't make his entrance until two minutes into the piece but he catches you from the first moment. His voice is emotional and yet completely unaffected – one of the greatest voices of tango. I cannot recommend him highly enough.

In the early 1930s, especially from 1932 onwards, Canaro's beat intensified greatly. "**Charamusca**" (1934) is a well-known example, but there are many others. Less intense, but still with a strong beat and also rather lacking the intimate feeling of the works with Charlo, are tracks such as 1933's "**Si yo fuera millonario**" with Ernesto Famá. This is exactly the formula to which Canaro would return in 1939.

Canaro: champion of the milonga, master of the vals

In 1932 Rosita Quiroga commissioned a milonga from the famous song-writing duo of Sebastián Piana and Homero Manzi. When the work was finished, she rejected it, but it was premiered to great acclaim by Mercedes Simone. Francisco Canaro then introduced "**Milonga sentimental**" to an unsuspecting dancing public. It was a success, and Canaro made it one of his specialities, recording more than fifty.

There are other orchestras that recorded a lot of milongas, such as D'Arienzo. In vals, however, Canaro reigns supreme, with more than 150 numbers to his name. Many of them are pure genius.

As with so many orchestras, our encounter with Canaro and his valses runs in reverse chronological order. His best-known vals (although not my own favourite) is the instrumental "**Corazón de oro**". There are two versions. The first to be reprinted, and therefore the more often played, is the 1951 recording which has an introduction and a chorus singing "ah..." in the background. I prefer the earlier, 1938 recording, which doesn't. Canaro also has some wonderful up-tempo valses with Francisco Amor at this time. I'm thinking of their interpretation of the Mexican song "**La zandunga**" (1939) and also their arrangement of "**Salud, dinero y amor**" (1939) which gives Enrique Rodríguez, who also recorded it, a run for his money.

A bit later we discover some of the valses with Maida: "**El triunfo de tus ojos**" (1938) and the immortal "**En voz baja**" (1937). These have a notably softer quality, as we would expect after what we've learnt about Canaro's shift of styles at the end of the 1930s.

Journeying back further in time, we come to "**Ronda del querer**" (1934) with Carlos Galán which belongs to the period with the strong beat just before Maida. The vals rhythm softens the hard beat making this a very satisfying piece.

I can't not mention the 1932 vals "**El jardín del amor**" ("The garden of love"). Canaro recorded this twice, but even the dance version comes in at over five minutes long, which just goes to show you what they could do in those days and destroys the myth that tangos were three minutes long because that was the length of a 78rpm disc. This vals is sung *a dúo* by Agustín Irusta and Roberto Fugazot – not in simple harmonies, but in a call and response fashion. The interplay between the voices is exquisite.

Now we've arrived at the years with Charlo. These early valses sound perhaps a little sparse to the uninitiated, but spend just a few minutes with them and Charlo's tender voice will overwhelm you. A super example is "**Con tu mirar**" (1930). This vals stands alone on the album on which we find it but there were many of them. Amongst my favourites are "Siempre te amaré" from 1930 and "Serenata maleva", "Florcita criolla" and "Ya viene el invierno", all from 1931. In these valses Charlo brings an intimate quality to the music. Emotionally they are more nuanced – neither the rip-roaring merry-go-round of his later work, nor the softness of the Maida years, but something more complex, with a feeling of yearning underlying the tenderness. I also must include "**Lirio blanco**" (1934) with a soaring lyrical vocal from Ernesto Famá, just to show that he could sound tender when Canaro gave him the right material.

I don't know quite what to make of the progression we've described. As we went back in time we first found simple, up-beat valses, then softer ones, and finally more nuanced and complex valses. I find the earlier ones much more interesting musically.

Canaro with Maida (1935 – 1938)

Maida has a velvet voice, and is one of the true greats – not forgotten today, but not nearly as famous as he would have been had he still been singing with a major orchestra when Troilo and Fiorentino re-defined the role of the orchestra singer. He is to Canaro what Héctor Mauré would be later to Juan D'Arienzo: a singer leading the orchestra on a more refined path that their band-leader just didn't want to go down.

We heard earlier how calm this can be when Canaro matches Maida ("**Poema**"), but even when Canaro is banging out the beat as for instance in "**Mano a mano**" from their final session together in 1938, Maida's honeyed tones damp Canaro's increasingly rough edges. This is something that we will miss greatly when Maida quits.

Canaro's populist era (1939 onwards)

The most charming of Ernesto's Famá's recordings in his second period with Canaro are undoubtedly those he made in 1939. Thereafter, our interest in Canaro largely collapses onto the milongas and valses. I just can't get excited about most of the tangos: especially in 1940-1941, Canaro sounds to me as if he's just going through the motions, even when he is giving such a great tango as "**En esta tarde gris**" its première.

Things improve in 1942 with the slowing of pace which that year brought and the introduction of two new singers: Carlos Roldán and Eduardo Adrián. Nevertheless, whilst there are some good numbers, the consistency that he had in the 1930s is no longer there.

Finally we have Canaro to thank for a handful of recordings that he made with the wonderful singer Nelly Omar in 1946-1947. Whilst Omar spent most of her career as a solo singer backed by guitars, here she sings as *cantora de orquesta*, orchestra singer. The arrangements are particularly rich, quite unlike the rest of his work from this or any period.

Six novelty numbers

1923: **Tutankhamon**. José Bohr became famous for the musical saw which he had discovered by accident in a friend's piano workshop. After hearing him perform this fox-trot Canaro asked him to come and perform it as a soloist with his orchestra. It sold 23,000 copies. When Canaro played in Paris in 1925 his brother Rafael doubled on musical saw, and other European bands such as the Viraldi Tango Band at London's Savoy Hotel followed suit. You can also hear a musical saw on Firpo's "Pilcha bruja" (1930) and on the Típica Brunswick's "La cumparsita" (1931).

Daniel Melingo reintroduced the musical saw on his 2009 album "Maldito Tango" and included it in his line-up on his tour.

1926: **Asserín, asserán** (See saw): No musical saw this time, but a *tango dialogado* – tango with spoken dialogue, one of a number recorded by the Paris based Bianco-Bachicha orchestra. This may have been the first such electrical recording, but the tradition is much older. Roberto Firpo's "Al gran bonete" (1920) sets to music a children's game, whilst Gobbi senior recorded a *tango dialogado* way back in 1907.

1933: **Milonga sentimental** (Sebastián Piana/Homero Manzi). Let's be honest: Canaro probably just tried this out as a novelty, but it was a hit with the dancing public and the rest is history.

1935: **Tangón** (Canaro/Pelay). Written by Canaro and Pelay for one of their stage shows, this rhythmical piece was quite forgotten until reprinted in 2003 by a small English label.

1939: **El rey del bosque** (The king of the woods): I can't help it, this Canaro tango makes me think of 'The Teddy Bears Picnic'.

1947: **Angelitos negros** (Little black angels): a tango about racism, the lyric was taken from a poem by the Venezuelan poet Andrés Eloy Blanco which inspired a Mexican film which was shooting at this time. This song is still performed today – for instance, it's part of the repertoire of Flamenco superstar Diego 'El Cigala'. You don't know him? Check him out – he's even recorded a tango album.

Francisco Canaro – plan of recordings (1926-1947)

With so many recordings and so many singers it can be hard to get a handle on Canaro's output. The following table shows the main years that each singer was with the orchestra, and whether or not we especially recommend them. The recommended years are shaded.

There will be good tracks in the unrecommended years as well, even some of our favourite ones – Canaro never lost his touch as a man who could read the public mood. This table is just to orient you to his most consistent work.

There may be some surprises in this table which can only be personal.

For instance, you'll see that I don't recommend Canaro instrumentals from 1936 onwards. That's right! Canaro was really strong in the late 20s and early 30s but now he just sounds plain without the soft voice of Roberto Maida. I also don't like Agustín Irusta's 1927 recordings, which is a pity because there are a lot of them. At this time Irusta sings with an exaggerated nasal tone – the style at the time, and probably a hangover from the pre-electrical era when singers had to sing much louder, but it hasn't dated well. The 1932 recordings sound more natural.

In summary: everything with Charlo and Maida is good, but with Famá stick to 1939 and earlier, except for milongas and valses.

If you want to find out which year a recording is from you'll need a discography. Christoph Lanner has an excellent one online here:

http://sites.google.com/site/franciscocanarodiscography/

Christoph has put in an enormous amount of work to prepare this discography, which is the best available. He does update it from time to time, at which point his index numbers change. Unless this system changes, this means one can't use his index numbers as a reference.

Francisco Canaro: plan of recordings (1926-1948)

Year	26	27	28	29	30	31	32	33	34	35	36	37	38	39	40	41	42	43	44	45	46	47	48
(Instrumental)	x	x	x	x	x	x	x	x	x	x	x	x	x	x	x	x	x	x	x	x	x	x	x
Agustín Irusta		x					x																
Charlo			x	x	x	x																	
Ada Falcón				x	x	x																	
Luis Díaz					x																		
Ernesto Famá							x	x	x					x	x	x							
Roberto Maida										x	x	x	x										
Francisco Amor														x	x	x							
Eduardo Adrián																	x	x	x				
Carlos Roldán																	x	x	x	x			
Guillermo Coral																				x	x		
Alberto Arenas																				x	x	x	x
Enrique Lucero																					x	x	x
Nelly Omar																					x	x	

Francisco Canaro: "La Cumparsita"

Canaro recorded "La cumparsita" a number of times. There were three early versions, in 1927, 1929 and 1933, all of them paired with "El entrerriano". When Odeón issued the new versions they gave them the same disc number (4262-B) and even re-used the same matrix number, #379, but with a suffix – normally used to indicate a retake. This has led to a great deal of confusion because it means you can't tell from the disc number what year the recording was made.

#379	17-02-1927	4262-B
#379/1	17-04-1929	unpublished ("inédito")
#379/2	17-04-1929	4262-B Serie sinfónica
#379/3	14-02-1933	4262-B Serie sinfónica
#379/4	14-02-1933	unpublished ("inédito")

Surely we can tell from the matrix number? The problem is that the suffix was mostly not printed on the label. Consequently, the most widespread version (the 1933) is nearly always misattributed to 1927. Nearly all the versions on CD are the 1933 version, whatever they say. The 1929 version (printed on CD by Blue Moon/el bandoneón) is very similar but can be recognised by the syncopation behind the bandoneón solo which starts at 1'00".

The hard-to-find 1927 version is quite different. It's taken at a much slower pace, sounds like a sextet rather than an orchestra, and when it gets to the minute mark, has not the bandoneón solo but the violin solo which becomes the final solo in the later versions (including D'Arienzo's).

Francisco Canaro: what to listen to

This is a bit difficult because the years before Maida are *very* poorly represented on CD. We've even been forced to recommend some mp3 albums. First of all, the really essential stuff:

mp3	Yesteryears	YY0172	Nights in Buenos Aires *	2010
CD	Euro	17049	"Pura Milonga" 1932/1934	2010
CD	Reliquias	235393	Canta Roberto Maida vol.2	2008
CD	Reliquias	541691	Sus éxitos con Roberto Maida	2003
CD	Reliquias	595159	Bailando tangos, valses y milongas	2003
mp3	Mundo Latino		The Roots of Tango: Desconfiale	2012

* This is an mp3 re-issue of the CD on ASV Living Era, 'La Cumparsita (1935-1940)'. The tracks cover the years 1935-1939 and have the best of Canaro's 1939 recordings.

Next, albums covering the best of the years 1940 onwards:

CD	Reliquias	541692	Sus éxitos con Ernesto Famá	2002
CD	Reliquias	235394	Canta Ernesto Famá vol.2	2002
CD	Reliquias	837414	Desde el alma	1996
CD	Reliquias	541690	Milongueando con Canaro	2002

There is plenty more Canaro from this period – check our website www.milonga.co.uk for further recommendations.

6/ Miguel Caló & Raúl Berón: to the beat of the heart

Listening guide

ORQUESTA MIGUEL CALÓ

1/ Al compás del corazón (1942) canta: Raúl Berón

2/ Ya sale el tren (1943) canta: Jorge Ortíz

3/ Si tú quisieras (1943) canta: Alberto Podestá

4/ Qué falta que me hacés (1963) canta: Alberto Podestá

5/ Mañana iré temprano (1943) canta: Raúl Iriarte

At the close of 1941 things were looking good for Miguel Caló. He had painstakingly assembled an orchestra of wonderful musicians – so good that it would later be called "The Orchestra of the Stars"; he had found and was nurturing two very promising young singers, Alberto Podestá and Raúl Berón; he had a radio contract; and he'd even finally been able to record again after a gap of over two years. Admittedly, only two 78s in the course of the year, but it was a start. Perhaps 1942 would be an even better year?

Suddenly, disaster struck. Carlos Di Sarli poached his best vocalist, Alberto Podestá, the one Caló had chosen for his recordings. Caló was angry, but what could he do? To sing with Di Sarli was a huge step up for Podestá, in both pay and prestige.

At the same time, questions were being raised at the radio station about the style of his remaining singer, **Raúl Berón**. His voice was a world away from the famous and successful voices of the day: dramatic, powerful voices such as those of Francisco Fiorentino, Alberto Echagüe or Roberto Rufino. With his smooth and velvety style, Berón's voice was more like that of a crooner – closer to Bing Crosby or Al Bowlly than it was to tango.

Miguel Caló was well aware that Berón's voice was different. He knew that it would need different material. And so in April he went for broke. He decided to take the risk of using one of his rare recording sessions to record Berón's voice singing a highly unusual new tango for which Homero Expósito had written the lyric. The arrangement was built around Berón's voice; smoother, slower and more romantic (but not in a lush or extravagant way) than anything they had tried before.

The innovative thing about this tango was the lyric. Instead of the familiar tango world of heartbreak and sorrow, it described a budding romance in terms of innocence, joy and hope. There had been tangos with positive lyrics before, but nothing like this, and the arrangement focussed attention on Berón's delivery. It sounds in fact as though Berón is standing right up close to the microphone, enabling him to croon very softly into the mike. It was a risk, and Caló knew it.

Caló's bosses at the radio station told him that he ought to sack Berón. Radio contracts were hugely important, and regretfully, Caló felt he had no choice. He told Berón that he'd have to go at the end of the month.

Then something unexpected happened: the disc came out and the new tango was a big hit with the public. A huge hit – much bigger, ironically, than it was for Carlos Di Sarli and Alberto Podestá, who had also recorded it. Almost overnight, everything had fallen in to place for Caló. Not only did he have a hit, not only did he have a singer, he had found his distinctive style: romantic and smooth, elegant and classy, but somehow still natural and fluid.

This new tango was called "**Al compás del corazón**", "To the beat of the heart", and it represents an evolution not just in tango but in the emotional life of a people and a city.

Berón, who'd been with the orchestra since 1939, spent the rest of the year with the orchestra, recording 15 immortal tracks before leaving to try his luck with Lucio Demare. That was a pity, even if he was to return in little more than a year, because the Caló-Berón team was on top form and had somehow really caught the mood of the public. The tracks with Demare are good, but not of the same class.

History has reasons to be grateful for the partnership of Raúl Berón and Miguel Caló. Without Berón the band would never have achieved the success and the fame which it won. If "**Al compás del corazón**" had failed, Berón would have been sacked and the band would have taken another, less adventurous direction stylistically, and with a different vocalist. Quite possibly we would remember it today as one of the less successful orchestras such as that of Ricardo Malerba.

Caló's other singers

During Berón's "year off" with Demare in 1943, Caló experimented with other singers. First he tried **Jorge Ortiz**, whose strong voice brought out another side to the orchestra. Ortiz stayed just six months and cut only seven sides but they have really stood the test of time: listen for instance to "**Ya sale el tren**" ("The train's leaving"), with fantastic work in the opening phrase from all the musicians but especially pianist Osmar Maderna as they imitate the sound of a steam train starting up. It's hard to believe that this is the same man who was the perfect voice for Rodolfo Biagi, and today we can only wish that Caló and Ortiz had done more together. Alberto Podestá also gets leave from Di Sarli (with whom he was not very happy) to cut a couple of recordings with the orchestra. Both are stunning: "**Percal**" and "**Si tú quisieras**".

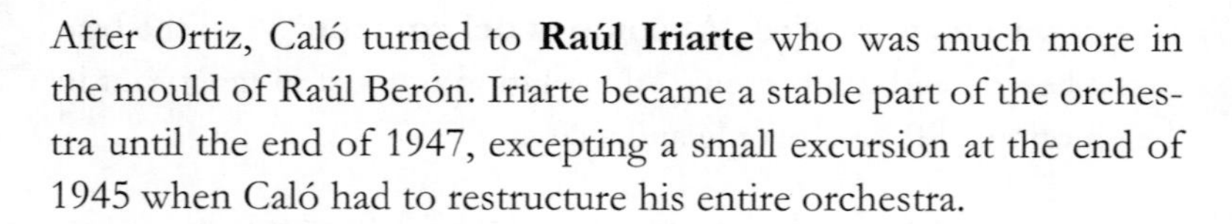

After Ortiz, Caló turned to **Raúl Iriarte** who was much more in the mould of Raúl Berón. Iriarte became a stable part of the orchestra until the end of 1947, excepting a small excursion at the end of 1945 when Caló had to restructure his entire orchestra.

The orchestra of the stars

Miguel Caló filled his orchestra with creative musicians, many of whom were also composers. It was nicknamed "The Orchestra of the Stars"; a lot of the band's material came from these men. Today this is the first thing we remember about his orchestra, but Berón's contribution is just as important. Without him, we wouldn't be giving the band nearly this much attention.

By the middle of the 1940s the tango scene in Buenos Aires was maturing. There were a large number of orchestras and a huge number of dancers, and many successful musical partnerships dissolved as people decided they wanted to make their own way, often with more individual music.

This is what happened to Caló's orchestra in 1945: his orchestra of the stars went supernova! First to leave was his pianist Osmar

Maderna, who ended up quitting over an argument, taking singer Raul Iriarte with him. This precipitated the departure of Caló's star violinist Enrique Francini together with his first bandoneón Armando Pontier, the two of whom had been thinking about starting their own venture for some time. In this case the split was amicable, but Caló had just lost his pianist, first violin and first bandoneón, along with one of his singers. However, he still had his arrangements. He put together a new orchestra with **Roberto Arrieta** on vocals which sounded remarkably similar, but although there would be hits later (such as 1963's "**Qué falta que me hacés!**", again with Podestá) the quality was mostly not the same. An era had come to an end.

We can only guess how satisfied the musicians were with their new ventures, but for dancers the results are not very satisfying. A case in point would be Osmar Maderna. His own orchestra showcased his piano playing in a way that we don't really enjoy so much today, but his contribution to the Caló sound was enormous. Listen behind the singer and he is doing a great deal – at the service of the orchestra. To listen for this, it's best to pick a track without Berón because the smoothness of both the arrangement and the very forward voice obscures some of what's going on. I'm listening to 1943's "**Si tú quisieras**" with Alberto Podestá who had returned briefly to the orchestra before splitting again, this time for Pedro Láurenz. The piano is everywhere between the phrases, with delicate, restrained fills, and just a little bit of rhythm. Not too much. This is Caló.

Like many bands, the Caló orchestra has a characteristic signature, a way of ending a piece, and in this case it comes from the hands of Osmar Maderna. Caló uses the delayed ending that we also see in Pugliese and Tanturi, not POM-POM, but POM – (pause) – pom. In this case, the second chord is given just to Maderna, who unleashes a small trill on the piano. Listen very closely, and you'll hear him then play one further chord, very quietly at the end. If you have a CD of Caló ripped to a computer, you can amuse yourself by listening to the end of any number of Caló tangos, all of them ending in this way: POM (pause) – prrom… ting!

Miguel Caló on CD: what to listen to

Everything from the Orchestra of the Stars period is worth listening to, although naturally it's the material from the early years which is best:

Reliquias	837413	Caló/Berón: Al compás del corazón	1996
Reliquias	499969	Sus éxitos con Podestá, Ortíz y Berón	1999
Euro	19015	Miguel Caló y Sus Cantores	2007

After this it's time to explore the tracks with Iriarte – half of which (the good ones) are with the Orchestra of the Stars (for instance  "**Mañana iré temprano**" with an exquisite piano introduction from Osmar Maderna) and half not. They are presented over two CDs:

Reliquias	837413	Sus éxitos con Raúl Iriarte	1998
Reliquias	499969	Sus éxitos con Raúl Iriarte vol.2	1999

Alberto Podestá returned briefly to the orchestra in 1954 and 1963 and the tracks Caló recorded with him provide the best of his output after the Golden Age. The quality of Podestá's voice pulls the orchestra up to another level. Some of the instrumentals are very good although not outstanding – you can hear those on this album:

EMI	371964	From Argentina to the World – Miguel Caló	2006

Miguel Caló discography 1941-1942

27	12.03.41	Yo soy el tango	Alberto Podestá	
28	12.03.41	Bajo un cielo de estrellas	Alberto Podestá	vals
29	31.07.41	Dos fracasos	Alberto Podestá	
30	31.07.41	Me casé con un sargento	Alberto Podestá	polca
31	29.04.42	El vals soñador	Raúl Berón	vals
32	29.04.42	Al compás del corazón	Raúl Berón	
33	30.06.42	Qué te importa que te llore	Raúl Berón	
34	30.06.42	Transnochando	Raúl Berón	
35	27.07.42	Tarareando	Raúl Berón	
36	29.07.42	Lejos de Buenos Aires	Raúl Berón	
37	02.09.42	Pedacito de cielo	Alberto Podestá	vals
38	02.09.42	Tristezas de la calle Corrientes	Raúl Berón	
39	09.09.42	Milonga que peina canas	Raúl Berón	milonga
40	09.09.42	Margarita Gauthier	Raúl Berón	
41	29.09.42	Azabache	Raúl Berón	candombe
42	29.09.42	Corazón, no le hagas caso	Raúl Berón	
43	09.10.42	Un crimen	Raúl Berón	
44	09.10.42	Jamas retornarás	Raúl Berón	
45	01.12.42	Milonga antigua	Raúl Berón	milonga
46	01.12.42	Cuatro compases	Raúl Berón	

7 / The two angels: Angel D'Agostino & Angel Vargas

Listening guide

Now it's time for a story that isn't full of twists and turns! This is the story of The Two Angels: pianist Angel D'Agostino and his singer Angel Vargas, who had one of the most famous and the most enduring partnerships in tango. Their beautiful and understated music is still a firm favourite with *milongueros* all over the world. Never have an orchestra and its singer been so closely identified. D'Agostino recorded so few instrumentals that people commonly refer to them in the same breath: D'Agostino-Vargas. It was years before I realised that D'Agostino led the band by himself.

They recorded 94 numbers in an almost uninterrupted run from 1940 to 1946. That's quite a record: none of the famous partnerships we've looked at so far cut so many sides.

In keeping with the simple story, the music itself is not ornate. It is understated, tasteful and subtle. D'Agostino avoids both the lush textures of Troilo or Láurenz and the edginess of D'Arienzo and Biagi, but still manages to be one of the most interesting orchestras rhythmically and lyrically.

If the rhythmic interest springs from the clean and simple elegance of D'Agostino's piano, the lyrical interest is largely in the voice of Angel Vargas. Like all the great singers, he wasn't merely content to perform the current hits but chose his repertoire with great care. Look at the discography and you may notice a very interesting fact: amongst those 94 numbers, there are only a handful that were recorded by other orchestras. This is pretty surprising. We know that the instrumental repertoire (e.g. of D'Arienzo) was different to the vocal repertoire (e.g. of Troilo), but D'Agostino/Vargas almost seem to have found a third strand. The repertoire is refined and nostalgic.

Listen to Vargas's voice and one can hear how he combines elements of both schools. He has the nasal voice and street phrasing of an Alberto Echagüe (D'Arienzo) or Alberto Castillo (Tanturi) but his elegance is matched only by Fiorentino (Troilo's emblematic singer). Vargas's style is masculine but his is not a "big" voice, and in this respect too he's a very good match for D'Agostino.

If you're just getting to know the music of D'Agostino/Vargas then the best place to start is with the tango "**Hotel Victoria**". We don't choose this recording for Vargas – he is quite simply perfect in all his recordings; we choose it because the arrangement gives much more space than normal to D'Agostino's elegant piano playing. The tango begins with D'Agostino's simple chords walking up out of the bass register. The other instruments slowly join in, but the opening sensitizes our ears to listen for D'Agostino's contribution.

When the second theme is introduced D'Agostino permits himself the most subtle of musical jokes: about 0'39" into the piece he joins the phrases together not with a trill or a run, but with a single note on his piano in a space which is otherwise held open and empty. It is a trick, but it's also characteristic of his style.

Once Vargas enters, D'Agostino links his singer's phrases with the most delicate of touches. The whole is possessed of a limpid clarity, like a river in summer. Throughout the tango there is delightful interplay between the instruments: for instance the trill in the piano which is copied by a pizzicato in the violin just before Vargas enters.

For a masterpiece of orchestration listen to "**Adiós Arrabal**". This is a delightful series of small musical conversations between the various sections of the orchestra:

A	violin – piano bandoneón – piano violin – piano orchestra – ***link***
B	bandoneón – violin bandoneón – violin orchestra – piano (x2)
A	Vargas – bandoneón (x4)
B	violin – bandoneón (x2) violin – bandoneón - piano
A	Vargas – bandoneón (x4)
B	Vargas + violin – orchestra Vargas + violin – piano

Interplay in D'Agostino's 'Adiós Arrabal'

Finally we should say that the music, whilst understated, is very interesting rhythmically from a dancer's point of view. D'Agostino commented in an interview that this is an aspect to which he paid careful attention, but the evidence of your ears is enough to know that this must have been the case. The music has playful *cortes* and some syncopation – all delivered with that characteristic restraint and subtlety. These qualities mean that the music is one of which you never tire, and this is one of the most popular orchestras in the traditional milongas of Buenos Aires, especially those taking place in the day time.

Vargas stayed with D'Agostino for six years (with a couple of little breaks) and the tracks from 1946 are very nearly as good as the first ones from 1940-1941. The sound of the music barely changes. Nevertheless, as ever, the earlier tracks have the edge.

Robert Duvall seems to be a big fan: he choose three D'Agostino-Vargas tracks for the soundtrack of his film 'Assassination Tango' – all of them from 1941.

D'Agostino after Vargas

Vargas's departure closes a monumental chapter in the history of tango music. D'Agostino finds good replacements and carries on; like Carlos Di Sarli, he remains true to his musical conception for his entire career and thus maintains his group as a dance orchestra right through the 1950s. If the later tracks lose a little of the subtlety of the earlier work then they have more force and they are still good for dancing, even though they don't have the voice of Angel Vargas. Rubén Cané has clearly been chosen because his voice is similar, whilst Tino García is a good choice as a contrasting vocalist.

D'Agostino-Vargas on CD: what to listen to

Happily these recordings are easy to find – but not always in the best fidelity. The best CDs yet released were the pair on the old 'FM Tango' label[10]. After these disappeared, the D'Agostino-Vargas 'RCA Victor 100 Años' album was a welcome and popular replacement, although with hindsight the transfers sound over cleaned.

There are four CDs on BMG's 'Tango Argentino' label presenting the 40s material and you should get them all, starting with volume 1.

Then there are three CDs on Euro Records to look out for. They all present a mix of 40s and 50s numbers but the place to start is the first one (EU-16011) which you'll find on their 'Archivo RCA' label. This takes you to the heart of their 1950s material – this album woke people up to the fact that for D'Agostino there was life without Vargas, another side to the orchestra. The album includes a pristine transfer of their astonishing 1955 version of

"**Café Dominguez**" – one of the only *glosas* recorded (the *glosa* is a lyric poem designed to be declaimed over tango music). As is usual, the *glosa* is not performed by the band's singer but by their announcer, in this case Victor Braña. (Sometimes you'll read Julián Centeya; he is the poet who wrote this *glosa*, and does not perform it).

---

[10] FM Tango was a tango radio station in the early 1990s. Both BMG Argentina and EMI Odeón Argentina produced a series of CDs under this imprint.

BMG	41291	Tangos de los Angeles - vol.1	1996
Euro	16011	Archivo RCA: Angel D'Agostino con Vargas y Otros 1943-1963	2009
BMG	41292	Los Dos Angeles - vol.2	1996
BMG	63357	Los Dos Angeles - vol.3	1996
BMG	63358	Los Dos Angeles - vol.4	1996
Euro	17012	Colección 78 RPM: Angel D'Agostino 1941/1953	2004
Euro	17027	Colección 78 RPM 2: Angel D'Agostino 1942/1953	2005

Be especially careful with the track "**No aflojés**". This is one of the few tracks that D'Agostino recorded twice, and the 1953 version with Rubén Cané is often mislabelled as being sung by Angel Vargas who recorded it in the band's very first recording session in 1940. Even EMI Argentina made this mistake on the 'FM Tango' CD. It's a sign of Cané's quality, and of the breadth of talent in Buenos Aires, that such a mistake is possible. Only Euro Records have this track labelled correctly (on EU 17012), and that transfer is on the playlist for this chapter.

8/ *Ricardo Tanturi: this is how tango is danced!*

Listening guide

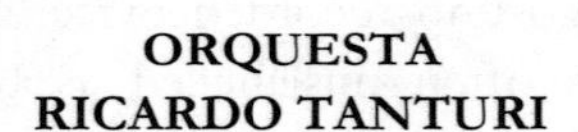

1/ Así se baila el tango (1942)
canta: Alberto Castillo

2/ Argañaraz (Aquellas farras) (1941)

3/ Oigo tu voz (1944)
canta: Enrique Campos

4/ Ivón (1945)
canta: Enrique Campos

Can you imagine the performance of a tango song causing a brawl? Well it happened – more than once, although like any good story, it has grown in the telling. The tango was "**Así se baila el tango**" – "This is how tango is danced" – and the provocative lyric was delivered by Alberto Castillo, the flamboyant singer of Ricardo Tanturi's orchestra.

Who was Tanturi, and what was special about his orchestra, apart from the fact that it was named after a polo team (Los Indios)?

Well, this is a good question, because there are a lot of things that Tanturi is not. First of all his is not a lyrical orchestra. It has the strong clear rhythm of D'Arienzo, but with less variation. Ricardo Tanturi leads from the piano but he's no virtuoso, and neither are his musicians. He keeps it simple. Tanturi's piano is strong and muscular – he really bangs it out! Compared to D'Arienzo, the bandoneón section is underpowered, so Tanturi keeps the *variación* short and gives more to the violins.

Perhaps because of this lack of virtuosity, Tanturi has other qualities – qualities which might bring D'Agostino to mind: a certain simplicity, and a respect for the melody. And it's this respect for the melody that saves Tanturi's music from being boring, even in the instrumental numbers, which admittedly he kept to a minimum – Tanturi recorded almost no instrumentals after the end of 1941. These early instrumentals such as "**Argañaraz (Aquellas farras)**" can be hard to find on disc but they are up-beat and exciting.

And when it comes to the vocal numbers, well, Tanturi has two fabulous singers.

The first was Alberto Castillo. This was how they came to meet. Tanturi was a dentist working in the Alvear Hospital. In 1941 he played at a ball there and his colleagues told him, you must hear this young medical student sing. His name was Alberto Castillo. Tanturi was impressed and signed him up.

A big personality, Castillo was first of all a fine singer with wonderful phrasing. His voice has that quality we call *canyengue*: street-wise and sassy, applied to a man's voice it implies a nasal tone. We said the same things about D'Arienzo's most famous singer, Alberto Echagüe, but Castillo has more flair and incredible phrasing. He really knows how to deliver a line. Troilo would later say that Castillo was the finest singer he ever heard – high praise indeed.

More than all this, Alberto Castillo was a natural showman, the very opposite of understatement. On stage, Castillo cut a virile and slightly swaggering figure, appearing in flash suits with wide lapels, always with a handkerchief in the top pocket, top button undone. As a performer, he was always engaged and communicating with the public, with exaggerated gestures. The overall impression was of a man of the street come good.

Castillo graduated in 1942 and began to practice as a gynaecologist. With his success in Tanturi's orchestra, he began a double life: Alberto De Luca, gynaecologist, by day, and Alberto Castillo, tango singer, by night. However, word soon got round that these two persons were one and the same, and Castillo found his consulting room full of ladies of all ages keen to be examined by the doctor. He was forced to quit his medical practice and dedicate himself full time to tango.

1942 was the golden year for Tanturi-Castillo, full of great hits. One of them, the one we most remember, was "Así se baila el tango" ("This is how one dances tango"). The lyrics praise the tango and those who dance it – at least, those who dance it well. They tell you how to dance it, and also how not to dance it. Castillo delivered all this with a flourish, leaving the audience in no doubt to which group they belonged – those who knew, or those who didn't:

> *What do those pretty boys know, slicked up, dressed up,*
> *What do they know about tango, about the beat?*

The lyric praises the real dancer whilst mocking the rich kids as empty suits. You can imagine that the effect produced depended very much on the delivery, and Castillo was a mischievous character. Those who saw him live tell that he would add gestures to the words, mimicking those who the lyric lampooned. One interviewer called it "throwing a rocket into a dish of spaghetti." Castillo naturally denied everything.

All publicity is good publicity, and Tanturi didn't mind the occasional spot of bother because the song was a huge huge hit. They recorded 37 numbers together before Castillo quit to go solo in May 1943. This turned out to be the right move for Tanturi, but it was not an amicable parting: Tanturi told Castillo that he would die of hunger. He was wrong: ever the showman, Castillo incorporated the *candombe* into his repertoire with a stage show of black dancers. It was a massive success, and Castillo became one of the most famous singers of his day. His fans followed him round like football supporters, on one occasion even blocking the street outside the theatre where he was performing.

Tanturi needed a new singer – fast. He organised auditions in which only one singer had the strength of character not to imitate Castillo's style. This was a young man from Uruguay called Enrique Troncone, and he got the job. Enrique had been performing under the stage name Enrique Ruíz, but Tanturi was worried that the public might confuse him with the many other singers called Ruíz. Opening a telephone directory at random, he chose the name **Enrique Campos**.

The second phase: Tanturi – Campos

Tanturi's instincts were right. Like Castillo before him, Campos also had a strong personality, but it was a completely different personality. It would require a change of direction for the orchestra which, not being built around virtuoso musicians, was particularly dependent on the singer for its quality. In stark contrast to D'Arienzo, who split with Héctor Mauré about this time and went back to a less sophisticated style, Tanturi embraces this change and a new binomial is born: Tanturi – Campos.

In Argentina, they say that whilst Castillo has the better voice, Tanturi – Campos is better for dancing. Why would they say such a thing? What is the change that Campos brought to the orchestra?

1942: the tipping point

By 1942 it's six years since the D'Arienzo explosion. Tango music has become more sophisticated but a big change happens in '42: the music begins to slow down. This is the year that Caló finds success with Berón, and Di Sarli is doing well with Podestá. A slower pace inevitably means that the rhythm is losing its pre-eminence; the melodic aspects are becoming more important. You can think of the years 1936-1941 as building the rhythmic foundations of Golden Age tango music. In parallel though, others have been preparing the melodic superstructure. The new year of 1941/1942 is a tipping point: from '42 onwards, the melody gains the upper hand.

This is not to say that melody and rhythm are in conflict, or that melody is *better* than rhythm. The melody rests on the rhythm, just as the torso stands on the legs.

Campos represents this shift within the Tanturi orchestra. Tanturi doesn't suddenly become a lyrical orchestra, but there is a shift. The texture of the orchestra thickens up, and whilst the rhythm is still there, the orchestra is more focussed on the melody. Campos's phrasing may be completely different to Castillo's, but like him he is concerned with delivering the lyric rather than showing off vocally. The orchestra has the same attitude: no pyrotechnics. The whole thing is completely at the service of the music. It sounds confident without being brash – mature. Campos is also very selective about his repertoire, much of which is unique although he does choose some of the same material as Chanel with Pugliese.

We have to say that the change is a triumph for Tanturi. He may have lost a star but the new combination suits the times better, and the orchestra continued to be successful, recording 51 numbers. Today Tanturi-Campos is even more popular for dancing than Tanturi with Castillo. The band displays the qualities that make it so good for dancing in tracks such as "**Una emoción**" and "**Oigo tu voz**". Compared to the earlier recordings with Castillo, the band still have a muscular sound but this is not just confined to Tanturi's piano. The violins have the same feel, and the whole texture of the orchestra has become more dense. Campos delivers the melody with strong character but also somehow with restraint. The overall effect is an unexpected coupling of strength and modesty.

Life in the orchestras of those days was a bohemian one, and in 1946, at the height of his fame, Campos retired from singing in order to have more time at home with his family, confining himself to playing the guitar. His replacement **Roberto Videla** sings well but cannot equal the character of the singers who preceded him. The real problem though is a small change in the music: Tanturi changes the way he makes some of his syncopations. This begins even before Campos leaves, for instance in 1945's "**Ivón**" where you can feel the missing note in the introduction, underneath the piano solo. Instead of **1 and (pause) 2**, we get: **(gap) and (pause) 2**, like this:

1	+			2				before 1945
	+			2				1945 and later

Tanturi: change of syncopation in 1945

What's the problem with this, isn't it exciting? The trouble is that it's too much of a surprise. Normally on beat 1 the orchestra make an *arrastre*, an acceleration that starts just before the note and attacks the beat. This tells you that the syncopation is coming. Without the first beat, the syncopation arrives without any warning. As a dancer, it's very hard to know that it's coming, so you can't react to it. This is a pity, because otherwise the music is still very fine. As it is, you never hear these tracks at the milonga.

Ricardo Tanturi on CD

TARG	41295	Tanturi/Castillo - Así se baila el tango	1996
TARG	41296	Tanturi/Campos - Una emoción	1996
TARG	63357	Tanturi/Castillo - Tangos de mi ciudad	1998
TARG	63355	Tanturi/Campos - Encuentro	1998

Tanturi: discography until the departure of Campos

1	23.06.37	Tierrita		
2	23.06.37	A la luz del candil	Ortega	
3	09.06.38	Carrasco	Ortega	marcha
4	09.06.38	Gallo ciego		
5	18.11.40	La cumparsita		
6	18.11.40	Argañaraz (Aquellas farras)		
7	08.01.41	El buey solo		
8	08.01.41	Recuerdo	Castillo	vals
9	19.02.41	La vida es corta	Castillo	
10	19.02.41	Mozo guapo	Castillo	milonga
11	06.05.41	Una noche de garufa		
12	06.05.41	La serenata (mi amor)	Castillo	vals
13	16.06.41	Comparsa criolla		
14	16.06.41	Pocas palabras	Castillo	
15	07.07.41	Lágrimas		
16	07.07.41	Mi romance	Castillo	vals
17	14.08.41	Noches de Colón	Castillo	
18	14.08.41	Adiós pueblo		
19	18.09.41	Didí		
20	18.09.41	Mi morocha	Castillo	milonga
21	27.11.41	La huella		
22	27.11.41	El moro	Castillo	
23	23.12.41	Recuerdo malevo	Castillo	
24	23.12.41	Ese sos vos	Castillo	
25	18.03.42	Al compás de un tango	Castillo	
26	18.03.42	Madame Ivonne	Castillo	
27	27.05.42	Así es la milonga	Castillo	milonga
28	27.05.42	Decile que vuelva	Castillo	
29	20.07.42	La copa del olvido	Castillo	
30	20.07.42	Voz de tango (tango)	Castillo	
31	14.08.42	Esta noche me emborracho	Castillo	
32	14.08.42	El tango es el tango	Castillo	
33	15.09.42	Cómo se pianta la vida	Castillo	
34	15.09.42	Marisabel	Castillo	vals
35	22.09.42	Muñeca brava	Castillo	
36	22.09.42	Un crimen	Castillo	
37	04.11.42	Cuatro compases	Castillo	
38	04.11.42	Recuerdo		
39	04.12.42	Así se baile el tango	Castillo	
40	04.12.42	Canción de rango (pa' que se callen)	Castillo	
41	04.12.42	Moneda de cobre	Castillo	
42	04.12.42	Me llaman el zorro	Castillo	

43	02.03.43	Qué podrán decir	Castillo	
44	02.03.43	A otra cosa ché pebeta	Castillo	
45	02.03.43	A mi madre (Con los amigos)	Castillo	vals
46	02.03.43	Entre sueños		
47	16.03.43	Ya sale el tren	Castillo	
48	16.03.43	Mi piba	Castillo	
49	29.04.43	La última copa	Castillo	
50	29.04.43	Que me quiten lo bailao	Castillo	
51	07.05.43	Barajando recuerdos	Castillo	
52	07.05.43	Bailongo de los domingos	Castillo	
53	06.08.43	Muchachos comienza la ronda	Campos	
54	06.08.43	Al pasar	Campos	vals
55	06.08.43	Vieja esquina	Campos	
56	06.08.43	Por eso canto yo	Campos	
57	09.08.43	Palomita mía	Campos	
58	19.08.43	Así se canta	Campos	
59	05.10.43	Dos palabras por favor	Campos	
60	05.10.43	Qué bien te queda (Cómo has cambiado)	Campos	
61	17.11.43	Oigo tu voz	Campos	
62	17.11.43	Una emoción	Campos	
63	17.11.43	Que nunca me falte	Campos	
64	17.11.43	Malvón	Campos	
65	16.12.43	Sollozos de bandoneón	Campos	
66	16.12.43	Qué vas buscando muñeca	Campos	
67	21.01.44	Rey de tango	Campos	
68	21.01.44	Quién canta mejor que yo	Campos	milonga
69	24.03.44	Y siempre igual	Campos	
70	24.03.44	Recién	Campos	
71	27.04.44	La abandoné y no sabía	Campos	
72	27.04.44	Y como le iba contando	Campos	
73	27.04.44	Desde lejos	Campos	
74	27.04.44	Jirón de suburbio	Campos	
75	18.05.44	Calla bandoneón	Campos	
76	18.05.44	Añoranzas	Campos	vals
77	27.07.44	Si se salva el pibe	Campos	
78	27.07.44	Sombrerito	Campos	
79	28.08.44	Domingo a la noche	Campos	
80	28.08.44	Desde el alma		vals
81	29.09.44	Encuentro	Campos	
82	29.09.44	El corazón me decía	Campos	
83	14.11.44	En el salón	Campos	
84	14.11.44	Prisionero	Campos	
85	13.12.44	El taita (raza criolla)		
86	13.12.44	Igual que un bandoneón	Campos	

87	22.01.45	Esta noche al pasar	Campos	
88	22.01.45	De seis a siete	Campos	
89	19.02.45	Me besó y se fué	Campos	vals
90	19.02.45	Qué será de ti	Campos	
91	12.04.45	Igual que una sombra	Campos	
92	12.04.45	La uruguayita Lucía	Campos	
93	03.05.45	Discos de Gardel	Campos	
94	03.05.45	Giuseppe el zapatero	Campos	
95	14.06.45	El sueño del pibe	Campos	
96	14.06.45	Anselmo Laguna	Campos	
97	13.07.45	Cantor de barrio	Campos	
98	13.07.45	Bien criolla y bien porteña	Campos	milonga
99	05.09.45	Ivón	Campos	
100	05.09.45	Cuatro recuerdos	Campos	
101	23.10.45	Cuatro lágrimas	Campos	
102	23.10.45	Tu vieja ventana	Campos, Videla	vals
103	09.11.45	Calor de hogar	Campos	
104	09.11.45	Tu llamado	Videla	
105	05.12.45	Corazoncito	Videla	
106	05.12.45	Este es tu tango	Videla	
107	03.01.46	Seis dias	Campos	
108	03.01.46	Soy muchacho del arrabal	Campos	
109	30.01.46	Barrio viejo	Campos, Videla	
110	30.01.46	Llévame carretero	Videla	
111	13.03.46	Así era ella muchachos	Videla	
112	13.03.46	Esta noche hay una fiesta	Campos	

9/ Rodolfo Biagi

manos brujas - enchanted hands

Listening guide

ORQUESTA
RODOLFO BIAGI

1/Cruz diablo ("Devil's cross") (1926)

2/ Racing Club (1950)

3/ Lejos de ti (v) (1941) estribillo: Teófilo Ibáñez
4/ La chacarera (1940) estribillo: Andrés Falgás
5/ Todo te nombra (1940) estribillo: Jorge Ortiz
6/ Humillación (1941) estribillo: Jorge Ortiz
7/ A la luz del candil (1943) estribillo: Carlos Acuña
8/ Pobre negrito (Flor de Montserrat) (m)
(1945) estribillo: Alberto Amor

1: piano solo
2-8: with orchestra

In November 1928, Maurice Ravel premiered a new work at the Paris Opera, his Bolero. Before the premiere, Ravel told a friend that the new piece was "not music" and predicted that orchestras would refuse to programme it. During the premiere a woman in the audience stood up and shouted "He's mad!" Ravel commented that she was the only person who had understood the piece. Despite this – or because of it? – it became hugely popular, Ravel's most popular work. The music is insistent, almost hallucinatory. With its nightmarish, tragic ending, it has been called a *Danse Macabre* – a Dance of Death.

It's embedded in our culture, and is still chosen regularly for performance: remember Torvill & Dean's "Bolero" and their perfect score at the 1984 Winter Olympics? Or perhaps you've seen Sylvie Guillem dancing Maurice Béjart's 2002 choreography? You only have to watch these performances to see what the dancers feel this music is about: eros and thanatos: the creative life force being confronted with the force of death. Sex and death.

I can't help thinking about Ravel's Bolero every time I hear Rodolfo Biagi's work. I'm thinking in particular of two instrumental pieces, works which bookend his career.

The first you have probably never heard of. It's his first recording, long before he played with D'Arienzo: a solo piano piece from 1925, his own composition: "**Cruz Diablo**" – Devil's Cross. It's the spookiest thing ever recorded in tango. Both in its title and its mood it gives a tango echo of Robert Johnson's famous blues "Crossroads" – but this is spookier. It gives me the creeps.

The second is from 1950, the Biagi orchestra's iconic recording of "**Racing club**". This is a very old tango given the full Biagi treatment.

Now what is the full Biagi treatment? Freed from the constraints of working with D'Arienzo (who ran a very tight ship), Biagi could do what he liked and you can hear that the rhythm is at once both more spacious – the texture is thinner – and more insistent. The *marcato* is amongst the most extreme in tango, as extreme as Pugliese at his strongest but because of the thinner texture it stands out more. Dare I say what I really think? It is *slightly mad*; but the ancient Greeks thought that artists were touched by madness, and you know what people say: the distance from genius to madness is a hair's breadth. Biagi was nicknamed *Manos brujas.* This is usually (and correctly) translated as *enchanting* or *spell-binding hands*, but the Spanish can be read differently. *Bruja* means witch. As an adjective it can mean *bewitching*, but the literal meaning is *bewitched*, as for instance in the ballet by Manuel De Falla, "El amor brujo" – "Love bewitched".

Manos brujas: enchanted hands. Genius and madness; eros and thanatos; sex and death. Tango. Ravel's Bolero; Biagi's "**Racing Club**".

Biagi put together his orchestra in short order after leaving D'Arienzo and his first vocalist was a veteran of the old guard, **Teófilo Ibáñez**, followed swiftly by **Andrés Falgás**. I love these early tracks. They are especially notable for the fast valses – an inheritance from D'Arienzo, who played a lot of valses and milongas to spice up the evening.

Being a highly rhythmic orchestra, Biagi now faced the same problem that D'Arienzo had before him: how to incorporate a singer when lyricism was not your priority. Listening to Ibáñez and Falgás, you can hear that Falgás's lyrical tenor is the better voice. His performances are more memorable. But despite this, he is not a  very good fit to the orchestra. In tracks such as "**La chacarera**" his voice floats above the orchestra – exactly the opposite of the effect that Biagi would ultimately develop. If anything, it is a step backwards for Biagi, not musically – the music is great – but developmentally. I love Falgás's voice but I wish that Biagi had persevered with Ibáñez, who disappears from view. It's as if, not quite getting the sound he wanted, Biagi takes a turn down a path which is not his own.

Luckily, Biagi did not spend too long in this musical diversion. In the summer of 1940, Biagi found the vocalist who would suit him best: Jorge Ortíz. In their first recording "**Todo te nombra**"  ("Everything names you") you can hear what made Ortíz such a good fit for the music as he effortlessly follows the sharp tumbling chords in the violins, hand in glove. Ortiz is able to fit around the choppy sound of the Biagi orchestra in a way that Falgás was not.

In these recordings Biagi starts to emphasise the off-beat in an extreme manner. This process reaches its climax with 1941's "**Humillación**", culminating in its fabulous delayed ending. A fun  game to play is to try and predict when the off-beat is going to come. Once you've got the hang of Biagi's style, you can start to guess where it might happen: the most common place is when linking phrases. Even so, it's impossible to predict 100% of the time without memorising the arrangements. This unpredictability is what makes the music so enlivening to dance to. It really makes you pay attention.

Now there's one more thing that I haven't pointed out. You remember how we talked about the rise of the *cantor de orquesta* in the 1940s, spearheaded by Troilo, whilst the star of the *estribillista* sets? Well, like D'Arienzo, Biagi is having none of this – at least, not yet. The times would eventually force D'Arienzo and Biagi to follow suit; but in "**Todo te nombra**", Jorge Ortíz is most definitely an *estribillista.* When the band has played the first verse and chorus, and we expect him to start singing – nothing happens! He comes in later and has less music to sing.

Perhaps this is why Ortiz quits in 1943 and goes to sing with – wait for it – Miguel Caló, who needed a replacement for Raúl Berón. It sounds unlikely, but to my ear it really works, giving Caló's music a bit of edge. Things didn't really work out for Ortíz though. Caló probably preferred a smoother voice, which he found within six months in Raúl Iriarte, and Ortíz eventually found his way back to Biagi. They would record 39 tracks together.

What to listen to

It's nearly all good, at least until about 1950, but the mood changes across the years.

The most accessible recordings are the early sides with Teófilo Ibáñez and Andrés Falgás. Biagi hasn't quite yet homed in on his own unique style but the up-beat tempo and the many valses and milongas make for a lot of dancing fun.

Then comes his best singer Jorge Ortíz. This is the Biagi sound at its most pure. The instrumentals are also very special; perhaps surprisingly, after recording many in his first years, there are none at all in the years 1943-1946 when the fashion for the sung tango is at its peak.

Appreciating the rest requires you not to insist that your Biagi is always up-tempo. This is something that many Biagi fans have difficulty with, but if you can get past this barrier, then it's possible to enjoy the music from later in the 1940s with vocalists **Alberto Lago** (1941-1942), the very fine **Carlos Acuña** (who also sang briefly with Di Sarli) (1943-1944) and **Alberto Amor** (1943-1947) – and I don't just mean the killer milonga "**Pobre negrito (Flor de**

Montserrat)". The final steps are to Carlos Saavedra ('46-'48), Carlos Heredia (just three tracks in the years '50 - '53) and Hugo Duval (1950 onwards).

In 1956 Biagi switched to Colombia where he recorded 20 more tracks, before recording a final LP on Music Hall in 1962. This period is quite forgettable – be careful because Hugo Duval is still on board.

Rodolfo Biagi on CD

Reliquias (the imprint of EMI Odeón Argentina) have done a good job of reissuing Biagi's recordings in good fidelity – there's no need to consider any other label.

Reliquias	499966	Sus éxitos con Andrés Falgás y Teófilo Ibáñez	1999
Reliquias	541689	Solos de orquesta	2002
Reliquias	379158	Exitos con Jorge Ortiz*	2010
Reliquias	499967	Sus éxitos con Jorge Ortiz vol.2	1999
Reliquias	499968	Sus éxitos con Alberto Amor	1999

* This is a reprint of the 1996 album 'Sus éxitos con Jorge Ortiz' with a subtly different title. Bizarrely, the earlier CD has been deleted.

10/ Enrique Rodríguez: cheerful tango

Listening guide

ORQUESTA
ENRIQUE RODRÍGUEZ

estribillo Roberto Flores:
1/ Tengo mil novias (v) (1939)
2/ Son cosas del bandoneón (1937)

estribillo Armando Moreno:
3/ Tango Argentino (1942)
4/ Amor en Budapest (fox-trot) (1942)

In Argentina, everyone dances everything.

Okay, that's obviously not true – certainly not today. What I mean is, go to a traditional milonga in Buenos Aires and the music is often punctuated by *tandas* (sets) of *otros ritmos* (other rhythms): swing, *"tropical"* (salsa, often with a tinge of cumbia) or even pasodoble. And when this happens many people are still dancing. These bursts of higher energy music keep the atmosphere light and playful.

Try this in Europe or North America and most people sit down. It's unusual there for people to dance tango, swing *and* salsa. Maybe this is why we have resorted to playing electronic tango or what people call "neo tango" – basically pop music with a 4 beat rhythm, to which it's possible to dance tango movements. Traditionalists (especially the young ones) hate this kind of thing but I wish they would just learn to dance a bit of salsa and swing. Then our milongas could become more like the parties they are meant to be.

Recently I heard Enrique Rodríguez's *orquesta caracteristica* described as a pop orchestra. What is an *orquesta characteristica*? It's a band that doesn't specialise in tango, vals and milonga, but plays all the other ballroom rhythms as well: fox-trot, pasodoble, polka, and others that are known in the Spanish speaking world but not the Anglophone such as *corrido*. Another such orchestra would be that of Feliciano Brunelli, although Brunelli performs very few tangos.

When I started dancing tango in 1994, Rodríguez's orchestra was one that you heard in Europe but not in Argentina. Being an *orquesta caracteristica*, I suspect they weren't really taken seriously in Buenos Aires. Admittedly their tango rhythms are quite simple but that's partly why we like them. The other reason is that the music is often, well, cheerful.

Their enduring popularity over here eventually led to more recognition in their homeland. You could get a CD of their music but it was mostly *otros ritmos*. It wasn't until 2000 that an Argentine label printed an album of Rodríguez's tangos. It's still very popular. Now nearly all of his tangos have been reprinted but he is still not well represented on the on-line listening services, and that has limited our selections for this chapter.

These reflections already tell you what you need to know about Rodríguez's orchestra. It's unpretentious, maintains a light feel, and just wants everyone to have a party. Sounds good to me.

Enrique Rodríguez – tango for pleasure

Rodríguez put together his orchestra in 1936, calling it "*La orquesta de todos los ritmos*" – the orchestra of all rhythms, and his recording career (on Odeón) begins in 1937. It's telling that he records a vals before he records a tango. Don't be surprised! This is an *orquesta caracteristica*, remember?

His first singer, with him until the end of 1939, was Roberto Flores, nicknamed "*El chato*". (If that sounds like a strange nickname – *chato* means snub-nosed – don't forget that Azucena Maizani was called "*la ñata gaucha*", *ñata* meaning much the same thing). Flores is a good match for the orchestra and these early recordings are up-beat, fresh and exciting. His most successful recordings were the fox-trot "**Amor en Budapest**" and the valses "**Salud, dinero y amor**" ("Health, money and love" – note the order) and "**Tengo**

mil novias" – I've got a thousand girlfriends – Rodríguez's own composition with lyrics from his friend Enrique Cadícamo. This vals, with its cheeky lyric, encapsulates what the orchestra was about, and introduces a factor that we might not associate with a Latin nation – irony:

> I have a thousand girlfriends, I am the champion of lovers!
> (chorus): *In your imagination!*

For a tango, try 1937's "**Son cosas del bandoneón**" – not as punchy as Biagi's later version, but still energetic and up-tempo. This is an enduringly popular tango.

At the beginning of 1940 the Victor label tempted Flores away to be a soloist and Rodríguez replaced him with Armando Moreno. Flores was a good match for the orchestra, but Moreno is too and he has a better voice. The new combination was even more popular than before, to the extent that Moreno was able to successfully perform songs from Flores's songbook. "**Tengo mil novias**" remained the orchestra's biggest hit although it's not true as we sometimes read that Rodríguez re-recorded this with Moreno on vocals.

As tango dancers we are most interested in the tangos. These were popular at the time and are just great for dancing. The music is interesting but not too sophisticated and has a gentle lilt. The mood is light and cheerful. Tango historians like to compare Rodríguez to other rhythmic orchestras such as Donato and D'Arienzo, but personally I don't see it. Rodríguez doesn't play with the rhythm in the same way. He does have rhythmic variation, but whilst Donato keeps you guessing, Rodríguez wants you to relax. As the pace of tango music slows in the early 1940s, the orchestra hits a sweet-spot in the years 1942-43 in which the tempo is just perfect for relaxed, enjoyable dancing. A typical example would be 1942's "**Tango argentino**". It's just a bit slower than "**Son cosas del bandoneón**" but this allows Rodríguez to use the music differently. Listen to this track and try to count it – is it a double time every beat, or not? This is just how Rodríguez uses the music, a very different quality to the fast paced double times of the D'Arienzo orchestra; these double times have a swing to them.

In the middle of 1944 Rodríguez decided that he needed to follow the trends of the time and make his music more sophisticated. He hired the pianist Armando Cupó and the bandoneonista Roberto Garza, both of whom were competent arrangers – Garza had already worked as an arranger for Canaro. The results are clear to hear in the music: their first recording, "**Motivo sentimental**" is certainly more complex. With its polish and sophistication it sounds like a different orchestra. This is a track that I associate more with the orchestra of José García and in fact at the start it sounds more like them than it does like Rodríguez. But when Moreno's voice enters, the game is up; neither José García nor Carlos Di Sarli would ever have used Moreno's amiable voice for this style of interpretation. Moreno just isn't a good fit to the "new" Rodríguez.

Not surprisingly you seldom hear these tracks at the milonga, especially the vocals. Instinctively we steer away from them, probably without realising what has happened. Rodríguez is trying to sound like someone else and it just doesn't work. No-one likes it, least of all I shouldn't wonder Rodríguez himself. Eventually he went back to his old style, and to his strengths, and everyone was much happier.

Rodríguez on CD: what to listen to

Quite simply, everything from the beginning (1937) until April 1944 is good, and that includes the fox-trots (of which there are many). If you are a tango dancer you may not think of yourself as someone who likes the fox-trot, but I'd encourage you to listen to Rodríguez's fox-trots – the ones from the earlier period. We've  selected "**Amor en Budapest**" for you to listen to – a massive hit for the orchestra. These fox-trots are always fun; some are absolutely outstanding. And if it's not too heretical a suggestion, you can dance a simple milonga to them.

Also don't ignore the recordings with Roberto Flores. Being from the late 30s rather than the 40s they are more upbeat than those with Moreno.

Once again, you can find (almost) everything on the 'Reliquias' label. For the tangos, valses and milongas:

Reliquias	541707	Canta Armando Moreno vol.2	2002
Reliquias	541704	Canta Armando Moreno vol.1	2002
Reliquias	477584	Sus Primeros Sucesos (canta: Roberto "Chato" Flores and Armando Moreno)	2005
Reliquias	595165	Tangos, Valses y Milongas	2003
Reliquias	541705	El "Chato" Flores en el recuerdo	2002

And for the fox-trots, these two early CDs:

Reliquias	837408	Bailando Todos Los Ritmos	1996
Reliquias	859024	Para bailar sin parar	1997

11/ Edgardo Donato: get happy

Listening guide

ORQUESTA
EDGARDO DONATO

1/ Tierrita (1934)

2/ Estrellita mía (v) (1940)
estribillo: Morales / Lagos / Gavio

3/ Triqui-tra (1940) canta: Lita Morales

4/ El adiós (1938) canta: Horacio Lagos

5/ Sinfonía de arrabal (1940)
estribillo: Morales / Lagos / Gavio

6/Felicia (1929)

7/El huracán (1932)
estribillo: Félix Gutiérrez

8/ Ella es así (m) (1938)
canta: Lagos

Enrique Rodríguez was not the only bandleader who simply wanted people to enjoy themselves. The other was Edgardo Donato. However, Donato's orchestra was not an *orquesta característica*, a pop orchestra like that of Rodríguez, but an *orquesta típica*, a proper tango orchestra – I would say, a serious tango orchestra, but the music that Donato makes is (mostly) anything but serious. Of all the orchestras who weren't afraid to make music that is simply happy, his stands out for its playfulness. You can hear this especially in the violins – Donato's own instrument – and in the bandoneón section, which has something different about it which gives the whole thing a Parisian *bal-musette* kind of feeling. The music is cheeky and upbeat. It has an innocent quality that we don't really associate with tango.

A great place to start is with Donato's interpretation of the tango "**Tierrita**", recorded in September 1934. The band takes the piece at a breakneck pace – it feels twice as fast as the recording made by the Orquesta Típica Victor (OTV) just two years earlier. The track opens with some frenetic guitar pizzicato on the violins (i.e. strumming the violin like a guitar). After a while things calm down a little, but only for some wild percussive syncopation to fill the background. Before long the pizzicato is back, and the piece carries on with this level of energy and excitement for the full three minutes. It's very dynamic, like a group of small children running around a playground. You can hear the influence on Tanturi's 1937 version (his very first recording) and yet Tanturi sounds sedate by comparison – and the OTV, pedestrian.

This child-like energy seems to be the key characteristic of this orchestra. Once when performing the tango "**El huracán**" ("The hurricane") Donato walked along the edge of the stage, smashing the stage footlights (coloured light bulbs) with the bow of his violin – presumably, in time to the music.

Consider what else was going on at the time and you can understand why some refer to Donato as a bridge to D'Arienzo, whose revolution is still more than a year away. Fresedo has already adopted the smooth sound of his years with Roberto Ray on vocals. Canaro is coming to the end of a three year period in which he championed the strong beat, and his orchestra is in transition; in just a few months time he will hire Roberto Maida. These two big orchestras are moving firmly in the direction of a softer music and the field is open for an upbeat orchestra. This is the gap that Donato fills. Canaro has a strong rhythm, Lomuto a heavy one, and Firpo a bubbling one: the Donato rhythm is light, quick and playful.

Donato's best years are 1932-1942, which is an odd range compared to the other orchestras we have been looking at. Clearly he starts well before the D'Arienzo revolution, so we might think of him as being a *guardia vieja* orchestra – albeit an up-tempo, up-beat one, but he keeps going very successfully after the D'Arienzo revolution, and even after the appearance of Troilo, Láurenz and Di Sarli. Why does he suddenly decline? Well, what happened in 1942? We discussed this when we were talking about Miguel Caló and Raúl Berón: the pace of tango music slowed down dramatically. Donato wasn't really able to adjust.

Something else happened to Donato around this time: he lost his key musician. We've seen that in many orchestras the key player was the pianist: D'Arienzo struggled at first to replace Biagi, and Troilo never really recovered from the loss of Orlando Goñi. Was it the pianist then? No, it wasn't. Try again. Could it be a violin player? Donato was well known for the particular way he used the violins – we've already heard his playful pizzicato. However, the man who often took the cheeky violin solos was Donato himself. Not the violin, then. A bandoneón? Warmer, but still not right.

Listen closely to Donato's bandoneón section: the sound is different to that of other orchestras. It's bright, happy and playful. How does Donato make it sound so light? The answer is that Donato's bandoneón section has an extra ingredient that that the others don't: as well as four bandoneóns, he has a piano accordion.

We're told so often about what makes the bandoneón different to the accordion, and so suited for tango: its sonorous depth, its melancholy. Well, just run this comparison backwards for a moment. The accordion is lighter and more joyful. Piazzolla said that the bandoneón was made to play sad music whilst the accordion is a very happy instrument. Donato, by adding the accordion to an *orquesta típica* line-up, is declaring his preference for the joyful in life.

The accordion player is the child prodigy Osvaldo Bertone, Bertolín to his friends. He joined the Donato orchestra in 1934 when he was just 13 years old.

Bertolín's contribution to the Donato orchestra was immense. At first he just lightens the sound of the bandoneóns, but as time goes on he takes more space, particularly in the valses, for instance "**Noches correntinas**" (1939) in which he has a simple solo. A more subtle example is "**Estrellita mía**" (1940), a medium-paced vals which features the trio of all three voices – at one point humming together in a most un-tango-like fashion! You don't need to listen too closely to notice something very unusual for a tango orchestra: one of these voices is female. This is the voice of Lita Morales. We'll come back to her shortly.

The best example of Bertolín's playing is the vals "**Mendocina**" (1942) in which you can hear his interventions from the very first bars. Maybe Donato gave him more space because he knew he was leaving, as this was cut on Bertolín's final session with the band. Listening to Donato's recordings, it may not be so easy to tell when Bertolín joins the orchestra, but it's very clear when he leaves.

The standard histories tell how Donato had to reorganise his orchestra in 1945 when many of the musicians, together with his singer Horacio Lagos, left to join a formation led by his brother Osvaldo. However the damage was done in 1942 when Bertolín, already eight years with the orchestra, left to form a jazz group. The last recording session with Bertolín – which includes "Mendocina" – took place in August 1942. Thereafter, and at the height of the tango boom, Donato recorded nothing for a year and a half. When he returned to the studio in March 1944 it sounds like another orchestra, lacking in personality. This is partly due to the loss of Bertolín, and partly due to the enormous changes taking place in the musical scene in those years, as the sung tango matured and slowed down – not playing to Donato's strong suit. There were other orchestras that failed to negotiate this transition, notably that of Roberto Firpo. Some would add to this list Canaro, at least from the point of view of his music rather than his success, but that's another story.

Donato anecdotes

Donato was famously absent-minded and stories abound about how he "lived in the moon". On one occasion he was chatting with friends in a *confitería* when he suddenly realised he had only a few minutes before his show began on Radio "El Mundo". Dashing out into the street, he jumped into a cab and asked to be taken to Maipu 555, as quickly as possible. The driver raised his hand to point out the building in front of them, saying: "It's here in front of you, Sir".

Donato found himself without a singer in his orchestra. One day he was at home, listening to the radio with friends. A singer came on whose voice really impressed him, and Donato leapt to his feet crying, That's it! That's the singer I need for my orchestra! An embarrassed silence descended on the room… no-one had the heart to tell him that it was Carlos Gardel.

On another occasion he sat down on the tram next to a lad carrying a violin case. After a while he turned to him and said, "Excuse me young man, do you play in any orchestra?" The boy replied, "Yes maestro, yours."

The most famous anecdote about Donato however is this one told by his daughter, which also takes place on the tram. Donato had become engrossed in conversation with a friend. They alighted together and walked on for a while before Donato realised he had forgotten something important on the tram: his wife.

Donato's beginnings

Donato makes his appearance in 1929 at a time when the *guardia vieja* is still the only one way to play dance music. The earliest recordings sound a bit like the Orquesta Típica Brunswick, especially in the way he uses the piano, but Donato is already showing his love of pizzicato: if you like, listen to his 1929 recording of "**Felicia**" which also has some nice syncopation.

In 1930 he co-led an orchestra with fellow violinist Roberto Zerrillo with singer Azucena Maizani on vocals, but Zerrillo fell in love with Maizani and followed her on tour to Spain. This forced Donato to go solo again.

In December 1932 he signed to the Victor label. The first session includes one tango, and the recording is a famous one: "**El huracán**". (The name means "The hurricane" but it's also a pun – this was the nickname of a famous football team). Listen to this recording and you can hear that the music is remarkably fully formed – it's an inventive up-beat tango that sounds just like the Donato we know and love and very little like the *guardia vieja* line-up with Zerrillo from the previous year. The piece really is like a hurricane, with wild dynamics that must have been a sensation at the time. This breakthrough tango became something of a signature piece for Donato and inaugurates his golden years.

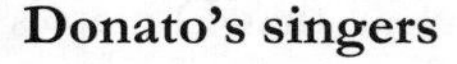

Donato's singers

Donato's vocalist on "**El huracán**" is Félix Gutiérrez, who apart from singing tangos was also a boxer. After Gutiérrez's departure Donato used Antonio Maida and then had the good fortune to premiere Hugo del Carril, who soon left him for stardom.

In 1935 he found the singer who would stay with him: **Horacio Lagos**. From 1939 he would make use of two other singers: **Lita**

Morales and **Romeo Gavio** (the Uruguayan Romeo Gavioli). It was very unusual to have a woman's voice in a dance orchestra. The solo tracks were given almost exclusively to Lagos although there is  one recording in which Lita Morales sings solo, "**Triqui-tra**" (1940). There is no other orchestra working with a regular female vocalist at this time: Donato is taking real liberties here. Mostly however Morales and Gavio appear combined with other voices – on five tracks all three voices appear together. This massing of voices adds to the party like atmosphere.

The serious Donato

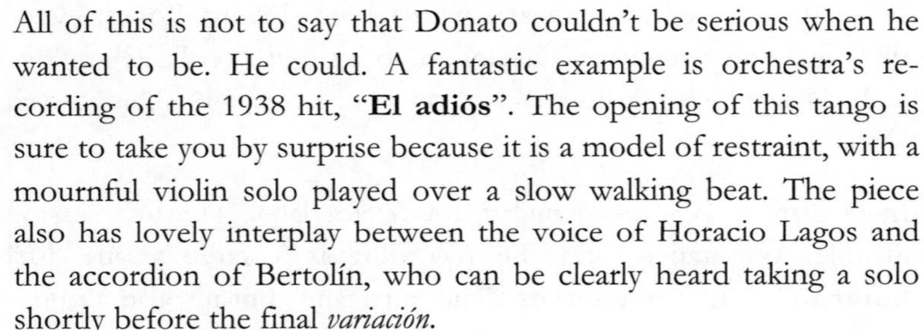

All of this is not to say that Donato couldn't be serious when he wanted to be. He could. A fantastic example is orchestra's re-  cording of the 1938 hit, "**El adiós**". The opening of this tango is sure to take you by surprise because it is a model of restraint, with a mournful violin solo played over a slow walking beat. The piece also has lovely interplay between the voice of Horacio Lagos and the accordion of Bertolín, who can be clearly heard taking a solo shortly before the final *variación*.

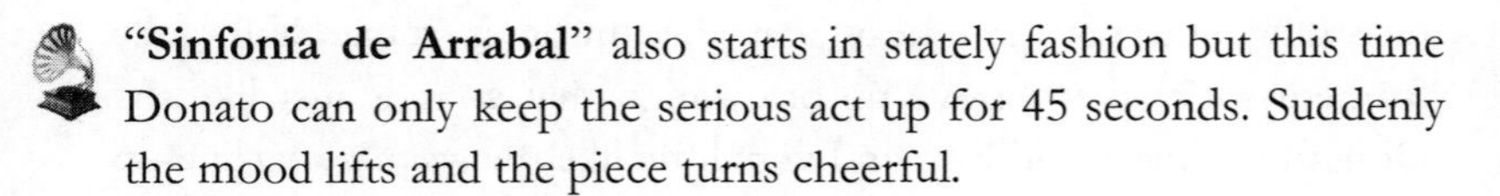

"**Sinfonia de Arrabal**" also starts in stately fashion but this time Donato can only keep the serious act up for 45 seconds. Suddenly the mood lifts and the piece turns cheerful.

Donato and milonga

Donato's cheeky rhythm makes him an excellent interpreter of milonga, his most famous today being the delightful if overplayed  "**Ella es así**". Listen to any of them and it's clear that Donato's treatment of milonga is a bit special, whether it be an up-tempo number or a slower one with the older rhythm we nowadays call *tango-milonga*. Donato himself struggled to find an adequate term to describe them, sometimes resorting to the made-up phrase *milonga tangueada*. This doesn't really mean anything except that we are somewhere in the territory between tango and milonga, but it does flag up a pitfall for tango DJs: Donato's rhythmic treatment of the

milonga is not always the same, so we can't just combine three at random and expect to make a satisfying *tanda*.

Donato on CD: what to listen to

Donato began on the Brunswick label, transferring to RCA Victor when they went bust in 1932. Of his 356 recordings, the ones which most interest us are the 152 he made with RCA Victor before the departure of Bertolín in 1942.

Sadly, BMG (owners of RCA Victor) have shown little inclination to reprint Donato's recordings and it has been left to the smaller record companies to bring us his music. At the time of writing there are just three commercial Donato CDs in print: two from Euro Records, and one from RGS. They are all outstanding, but between them they give us only 65 of the 156 recordings we really want to have. Many classic tracks are simply unavailable on commercially released CDs. It would be lovely if this had changed by the time you read this, but the chances are slim.

Euro	17019	Colección 78 RPM: Edgardo Donato 1933/1941	2004
Euro	17025	Colección 78 RPM 2: Edgardo Donato 1938/1942	2005
RGS	1640	Tango Collection: Edgardo Donato	2010

Edgardo Donato – partial discography

135	09.12.32	El huracán	Félix Gutiérrez	
136	09.12.32	Adónde vas tan regalón?	Félix Gutiérrez	ranchera
137	21.06.33	La llorona	Félix Gutiérrez	ranchera
138	21.06.33	Pobre soñador	Félix Gutiérrez	
139	13.07.33	La novena	Félix Gutiérrez; Manuel Cao	
140	13.07.33	Veneración		vals
141	11.09.33	Triste y sin alpiste	Félix Gutiérrez	ranchera
142	11.09.33	El acomodo		
143	31.10.33	Mi porteñita grácil	Félix Gutiérrez	pasodoble
144	31.10.33	Santa milonguita	Félix Gutiérrez	
145	29.11.33	Penas	Félix Gutiérrez	vals
146	29.11.33	Qué haces, qué haces	Félix Gutiérrez	
147	09.01.34	Esto es el colmo	Antonio Maida	
148	09.01.34	Petronila y Candelario	Antonio Maida	ranchera
149	09.02.34	Ruego	Antonio Maida; "Randona"	
150	09.02.34	Abombada	Randona	ranchera
151	12.03.34	Noche sevillana	Antonio Maida	pasodoble
152	12.03.34	Risas	Antonio Maida	
153	25.04.34	Sandia calada	Antonio Maida	ranchera
154	25.04.34	Seguí la caravana	Antonio Maida	
155	05.06.34	Amores viejos	Antonio Maida	
156	05.06.34	Pa' semejante candil	Antonio Maida	ranchera
157	28.06.34	Riachuelo	Antonio Maida; "Randona"	
158	28.06.34	Ensalada mixta	Antonio Maida	ranchera
159	28.06.34	Y llegó el amor	Antonio Maida	vals
160	28.06.34	Berretín	Antonio Maida	
161	09.08.34	Una luz en tus ojos	Antonio Maida; "Randona"	vals
162	09.08.34	Soldadito del amor	Antonio Maida	pasodoble
163	14.09.34	Ladrona de Sevilla	Antonio Maida	pasodoble
164	14.09.34	Tierrita		
165	05.10.34	Corrales viejos	Antonio Maida	milonga
166	05.10.34	Miau	Antonio Maida	ranchera
167	09.11.34	Quién más, quién menos	Antonio Maida; "Randona"	
168	08.11.34	Rosiclor	Antonio Maida	vals
169	19.12.34	De ande yerba	Antonio Maida	ranchera
170	19.12.34	Si te perdés, chiflame	Antonio Maida	
171	05.02.35	Protestona	Antonio Maida	ranchera
172	05.02.35	La caída de la estantería	Hugo Del Carril	
173	08.02.35	Congoja	Hugo Del Carril	

174	08.02.35	La glotona	Antonio Maida	ranchera
175	20.02.35	Dejate querer		vals
176	20.02.35	Madame Ivonne	Alberto Gómez	
177	21.03.35	Rosa poneme una ventosa	Hugo Del Carril; "Randona"	
178	21.03.35	Vos y yo	Hugo Del Carril	vals
179	04.04.35	Muchacho de cafetín	Hugo Del Carril	
180	04.04.35	El vals de los recuerdos	Hugo Del Carril	vals
181	06.05.35	La cumparsita		
182	06.05.35	Mi morena	Hugo Del Carril; "Randona"	pasodoble
183	06.05.35	San Sebastián	Hugo Del Carril	pasodoble
184	06.05.35	Mi tristeza	Hugo Del Carril	
185	13.06.35	Dios lo sabe	Juan Alesio	
186	13.06.35	El día que me quieras	Juan Alesio	canción
187	03.07.35	Rosalinda	Juan Alesio	vals
188	03.07.35	Picaflor	Juan Alesio	
189	17.07.35	De mis pagos		ranchera
190	17.07.35	Hola... ¿Qué tal?	Juan Alesio	
191	09.08.35	Lejana tierra mía	Juan Alesio	canción
192	09.08.35	Alleluia	Juan Alesio	marcha
193	28.08.35	El zorzal	Horacio Lagos	
194	28.08.35	Doña Maribiga	Horacio Lagos	ranchera
195	11.10.35	Hay que acomodarse	Horacio Lagos	
196	11.10.35	Mi Sevilla		pasodoble
197	20.11.35	Elegante papirusa		
198	20.11.35	Che, Carolina		ranchera
199	17.01.36	Tengo flor y no la niego	Horacio Lagos	ranchera
200	17.01.36	Chiqué		
201	10.03.36	Mañana	Félix Gutiérrez	
202	10.03.36	La tapera	Félix Gutiérrez	vals
203	07.05.36	Secreto de amor	Félix Gutiérrez	vals
204	07.05.36	Pura chispa	Félix Gutiérrez	
205	10.06.36	Embrujo gitano	Horacio Lagos	pasodoble
206	10.06.36	Belén		
207	01.07.36	Si tu supieras	Horacio Lagos	
208	01.07.36	Sólo un recuerdo	Horacio Lagos	vals
209	06.08.36	Gallito		pasodoble
210	06.08.36	La tablada		
211	10.09.36	Me voy a baraja	Horacio Lagos	
212	10.09.36	Sombras del ayer	Horacio Lagos	vals
213	07.10.36	Se va la vida	Horacio Lagos	
214	07.10.36	Adiós a Gardel	Horacio Lagos	corrido
215	23.01.37	Pierrot apasionado	Horacio Lagos	marcha
216	23.01.37	No te cases	Horacio Lagos	
217	12.02.37	Así es el tango	Horacio Lagos	

218	12.02.37	Gato	Horacio Lagos	
219	16.07.37	Marta	Horacio Lagos	vals
220	16.07.37	Hacete cartel	Horacio Lagos	
221	29.11.37	Papas calientes		tango milonga
222	29.11.37	Virgencita	Horacio Lagos	vals
223	05.02.38	El estagiario		
224	05.02.38	La milonga que faltaba	Horacio Lagos	milonga
225	09.03.38	Qué sera?	Horacio Lagos	vals
226	09.03.38	Sácale punta	Horacio Lagos; "Randona"	milonga
227	02.04.38	El adiós	Horacio Lagos	
228	02.04.38	Con tus besos	Horacio Lagos	vals
229	06.07.38	Tiempos bravos		
230	06.07.38	Te gané de mano	Horacio Lagos; "Randona"	
231	29.08.38	Vivo sin sombra lejos de ti	Horacio Lagos	vals
232	29.08.38	Cantando bajito	Horacio Lagos	
233	10.10.38	Ella es así	Horacio Lagos	milonga
234	10.10.38	El chamuyo		
235	09.12.38	Alas rotas	Horacio Lagos	
236	09.12.38	Embrujo		pasodoble
237	26.01.39	La mimada	Horacio Lagos	milonga
238	26.01.39	Para qué	Horacio Lagos	
239	06.03.39	Lágrimas	Horacio Lagos	
240	06.03.39	De punta a punta	Horacio Lagos	milonga
241	27.03.39	Carnaval de mi barrio	Lagos; Morales	
242	27.03.39	Madrecita	Horacio Lagos	vals
243	27.03.39	Sombra gaucha	Morales; Lagos	
244	05.06.39	Sin sabor	Lagos; Morales	
245	02.08.39	Pasión criolla		
246	02.08.39	Trinia	Lita Morales	pasodoble
247	31.08.39	Chapaleando barro	Lagos; Morales	
248	31.08.39	Soy mendigo	Horacio Lagos	
249	14.11.39	El torito		milonga
250	14.11.39	Noches correntinas	Morales; Lagos; Gavio	vals
251	11.01.40	Mi serenata	Gavio; Morales	
252	11.01.40	Volverás pero cuándo	Gavio; Morales; Lagos	vals
253	24.01.40	Luna	Gavio; Morales; Lagos	vals
254	24.01.40	Triqui-tra	Lita Morales	
255	05.04.40	Campo afuera	Horacio Lagos	milonga
256	05.04.40	Sinfonía de arrabal	Lagos; Morales;	

			Gavio	
257	30.04.40	La melodía del corazón	Romeo Gavio	
258	30.04.40	Porteña linda	Horacio Lagos	milonga
259	18.07.40	El distinguido ciudadano		
260	18.07.40	Diablesa	Horacio Lagos	vals
261	30.09.40	Estrellita mía	Morales; Lagos; Gavio	vals
262	30.09.40	Yo te amo	Morales; Gavio	
263	22.11.40	Fue mi salvación	Horacio Lagos	
264	22.11.40	Virgencita milagrosa	Lita Morales	pasodoble
265	13.12.40	El lengue	con recitado	milonga
266	13.12.40	Sentir del corazón	Horacio Lagos; Romeo Gavio	milonga
267	21.01.41	Dejá el mundo como está	Horacio Lagos	
268	21.01.41	La shunca	Gavio; Morales; Lagos	vals
269	05.02.41	La morena de mi copla	Lita Morales	pasodoble
270	05.02.41	Amando en silencio	Lagos; Gavio	
271	18.02.41	Mis pesares	Horacio Lagos	
272	18.02.41	Repique del corazón	Lagos; Gavio	milonga
273	11.06.41	Organillero	Horacio Lagos	marcha
274	11.06.41	A oscuras	Horacio Lagos	
275	21.07.41	Te busco	Horacio Lagos	
276	21.07.41	No se haga mala sangre	Horacio Lagos	polca
277	06.08.41	Un libro	Horacio Lagos	
278	06.08.41	Mañana sera la mía	Lagos; Morales	vals
279	13.10.41	A media luz	Horacio Lagos	
280	13.10.41	Quién será	Horacio Lagos	vals
281	11.03.42	Cara negra	Horacio Lagos	milonga
282	11.03.42	Mishiadura		
283	28.05.42	Parece ayer	Horacio Lagos	
284	28.05.42	Tu confidencia	Romeo Gavio	
285	06.08.42	Mendocina	Romeo Gavio	vals
286	06.08.42	Lonjazos	Gavio; Lagos	

Note: The singer "Randona" – sometimes to be heard singing a high falsetto *a dúo* with Donato's main singer Antonio Maida – was Donato's violinist Armando Julio Piovani.

12/ Elvino Vardaro:

the greatest orchestra there never was

If someone is merely ahead of his time, it will catch him up one day

- Ludwig Wittgenstein

Listening guide

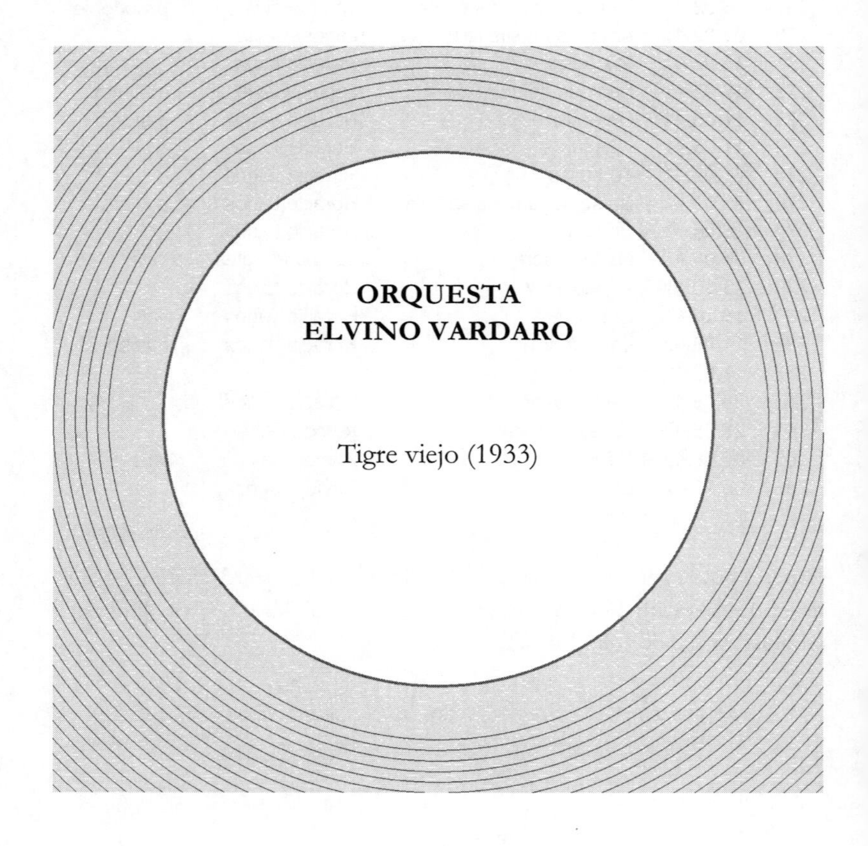

Elvino Vardaro was one of the best tango violinists of all time. The list of people he played with is a veritable 'Who's Who' of tango. Beginning with Juan Maglio in 1922, he also played with the sextets of Roberto Firpo (1924) and Pedro Maffia (1926), as well as playing with all the artists of the Victor company in the late 20s: Juan Guido, Ciriaco Ortiz's Los Provincianos, Luis Petrucelli, Adolfo Carabelli and of course Victor's house orchestra, the Orquesta Típica Victor (OTV) itself. Later he played for both Fresedo and Di Sarli.

In 1929 he formed the now mythical Vardaro-Pugliese sextet which had Malena de Toledo (considered by some to be the muse of the iconic tango "Malena") as vocalist. Vardaro assembled the best young musicians of his day into a line-up that with hindsight one might consider the greatest ever. Osvaldo Pugliese was on piano. The bandoneón players were Aníbal Troilo and Ciriaco Ortiz. The second violin was Alfredo Gobbi. Including himself, every one of these six musicians would eventually lead their own orchestra. The next time anything comparable would happen would be the Quinteto Real in 1960.

This sextet did well and decided to tour Argentina. Unfortunately this tour was a complete failure. Vardaro had to pawn his violin to pay for the tickets home and the group broke up without leaving any recordings.

Not to be put off, in 1933 Vardaro formed his own sextet. With Vardaro on first violin, Troilo was one of the bandoneóns. The other violin was Hugo Baralis, who would later play for Troilo. Vardaro did the arrangements along with the pianist, José Pascual.

The group left only one recording: a test recording cut for Victor in 1933 of the tango "**Tigre Viejo**". This is one of the outstanding recordings of the whole tango era. The arrangement eschews conventional notions of how to perform a tango. The music is a series of wild, abandoned flourishes. By comparison, Fresedo's recording of "Tigre viejo" – one of his most rhythmic – sounds not simply staid and effeminate, but emasculated.

This test recording was turned down by Victor on the grounds that the music was not commercial.

The group was hugely popular in their public performances. They were resident at the Café Germinal where they were nicknamed the Sexteto Germinal. But success needed more: a radio contract and a recording contract. Without either of these there was no financial future for the group and they broke up in 1935 without making any commercial recordings.

Horacio Ferrer calls this group an anticipation of Troilo. Whilst I can see that the Vardaro sextet was the bridge between De Caro and Troilo, I can't see it as a precursor of Troilo. The musical conception of the group is different, reminding one much more of Láurenz. It's the closest thing to jazz that tango has to offer: six men playing on the edge of their seats, and just about keeping the whole thing on the rails.

The test recording remained I believe not with Vardaro but with the band's second bandoneón Jorge Fernández and was kept by his family after his death. Not knowing how to look after it, they decided to preserve it by covering it in olive oil. Eventually it was brought to a private collector who cleaned off the oil by bathing it in vaseline (!) and made the transfer, which he circulated amongst other collectors. It has now "escaped" onto a commercial mp3.

What happened to Vardaro? In 1938 he briefly co-led an orchestra with Lucio Demare. After this he led a jazz orchestra for a time. Then he played in the orchestras of Adolfo Pérez, Osvaldo Fresedo and Joaquin do Reyes. By the time he reformed an orchestra in 1944 the moment had passed. The resurgence of the ideas he championed would have to wait for the emergence of a member of the Decarean school: Pedro Láurenz.

13 / Pedro Láurenz: The herald of the Golden Decade

Listening guide

ORQUESTA PEDRO LÁURENZ

1/Arrabal (1937)

canta Héctor Farrel
2/Abandono (1937)

canta Juan Carlos Casas:
3/No me extraña (1940) 4/Mascarita (v) (1940)

canta Martín Podestá:
5/ La vida es una milonga (m) (1941)

canta Alberto Podestá:
6/Nunca tuvo novio (1943)
7/Alma de bohemia (1943)

canta Carlos Bermúdez:
8/Más solo que nunca (1944)

Let's start with a wild claim: if D'Arienzo was the person who made the Golden Age possible, then the man who inaugurated it was Pedro Láurenz.

Now what can I mean by this?! D'Arienzo was the man who had propelled a city to its feet. However there's another view of Juan D'Arienzo in Argentina that we've only hinted at so far. His music split opinion and it continues to do so today. The appreciation of his music is shall we say reluctant amongst the Argentine intelligentsia. Many see his music as a backward step in the development of tango, and this opinion is still widely held. Here for instance are the published views of José Gobello (Argentine writer and expert in lunfardo), quoted on the leading tango website in Argentina[11]:

> *Tango lovers despise D'Arienzo. He is considered as a sort of tango demagogue.*

And things are hardly helped when, in the next paragraph, he answers Piazzolla's complaint that people like the old music ("the music of the dead") by saying you can't blame children for liking children's books. One wonders who is to be considered a tango lover when millions of tango dancers appear not to count?

But give the devil his due… to get an idea what the critics are complaining about, let's go to the year 1937. D'Arienzo is at the height of his fame, with Biagi in the pianist's chair; neither Troilo nor Pugliese has appeared, and Di Sarli is still in a self-imposed exile. D'Arienzo is riding high. This is the moment when Pedro Láurenz makes his first recording, an interpretation that was so inventive, it must have exploded into the musical scene of Buenos Aires like a grenade, even if it didn't sell a lot of discs. That recording was "**Arrabal**".

[11] http://www.todotango.com/english/creadores/jdarienzo.html (accessed: 20th June 2012). Originally published in Tango y Lunfardo Nº 132, Year XIV, Chivilcoy, 16 September 1997

Tangos which defined history

No, we're not talking about "La cumparsita" or the first tango sung by Gardel, "Mi noche triste" – we're talking about the works which broke new ground musically.

1897: **El entrerriano** (Rosendo Mendizábal). Whilst it's not quite true that this is the first structured tango – Prudencio Aragón had premiered **El talar** c. 1894 – Mendizábal's work is the one everyone remembers. This tango had incredibly broad appeal: it was performed by D'Arienzo, Biagi, Firpo, Canaro, Maffia, Fresedo, De Angelis, Troilo and Pugliese. Both works have the structure ABACA.

According to legend, this is the tango that was played during that famous evening in 1912 when Argentine playboy Ricardo Guiraldes stunned the Parisian smart set by dancing a tango at a fashionable Parisian salon.

It was followed by **Don Juan** (Ernesto Ponzio 1898) – the first tango recorded by a tango orchestra (Greco in 1911). In the same mould we find **El choclo** (Angel Villoldo 1903) and the more melodious **La morocha** (Enrique Saborido / Angel Villoldo 1905). All of these still form part of the standard repertoire.

1909: **Ojos Negros** (Vicente Greco). Anyone who has heard Troilo's 1950s recording of this work might find it hard to believe that it was written so early. Ojos Negros prefigures the changes to come. The piece has a strong melody (allegedly given to Greco by his friend Prudencio Aragón) with a sentimental feeling to which Greco added the canyengue backing of the 2 x 4.

1914: **Alma de bohemio** (Roberto Firpo). The sheet music cover says, "Tango de Concierto" – a concert tango. Firpo wrote this for the stage which gave him the freedom to write a lyrical piece with an emotional air.

1917: **Gallo ciego** (Agustín Bardi). One of the tangos which defined the change to the 4 x 8, Gallo ciego was not just taken on by D'Arienzo and Tanturi, who both recorded this pillar of the guardia vieja repertoire, but its repetitive structure is a clear inspiration to the work of Osvaldo Pugliese who recorded it in 1959. The other tango defining that change is Eduardo Arolas's **Comme il faut** (1917), recorded three times by Di Sarli. Both are structured around crisp eighth notes.

1917: **Sans souci** (Enrique Delfino). A new kind of tango, the romantic tango ("tango romanza") followed in the line of development established by Firpo in **Alma de bohemio**. Juan Carlos Cobián develops similar ideas at the same time but this is the tango that won its place in the repertoire. The piece is named after a perfume launched by Yardley the same year.

1921: **La cachila** (Eduardo Arolas). This beautiful melody is definitely in 4 but its longer phrase points towards the 4 x 4. La cachila synthesizes the romantic tango of Delfino and Cobián with the 4 x 8 of Arolas and Bardí. This tango is the end of the *guardia vieja*.

1926?: **Recuerdo** (Osvaldo Pugliese). The birth of the 4 x 4, this tango nevertheless retains a strong rhythmic pulse which makes it wonderful for dancing.

1927: **Flores negras** (Francisco De Caro). One of the most beautiful melodies ever written for tango, exquisitely phrased and harmonised. The melody is in control of this piece, not the rhythm. This is the manifesto of the 4 x 4 movement.

1934: **Arrabal** (José Pascual). From the dancer's point of view one of the greatest tangos ever written.

1946: **La yumba** (Osvaldo Pugliese). Pugliese resurrects the ideas behind Bardi's **Gallo ciego** to create his master work.

Láurenz was in the studio on 24th September, 1937. Just for fun, let's see what D'Arienzo was recording around that time. As luck would have it, D'Arienzo was in the studio just two days earlier recording "El caburé" and "Milonga vieja milonga".

Compare these recordings and "**Arrabal**" is a runaway winner. From the opening notes – a wild flourish on the bandoneóns – this is simply at another level. The music effervesces with creativity and invention. D'Arienzo may be King of the Beat, but Láurenz has a thing or two to teach him about rhythm as he switches effortlessly in and out of strongly syncopated 3-3-2 rhythms that just drive dancers crazy.

Now before I get too carried away, let's remember that much of the genius of this recording comes from the composer of "Arrabal", José Pascual, the pianist in Vardaro's vanished sextet. When was the piece written? "Arrabal" was a sensation in 1937, but in fact it was composed back in 1934. Vardaro performed it at Café Germinal. The bandoneonista Andrés Natale remembers hearing them play at the Germinal in 1934, when he was just 9 years old. Watching the boy fingering chords on the bandoneón, Troilo came over to help him, and José Pascual gave him the sheet music for "Arrabal"[12]. Another person who heard the Vardaro "Arrabal" was a young Astor Piazzolla, who vividly recalled hearing the sextet on a radio broadcast in May 1938[13]. He describes the interpretation in Spanish as *"celestial"* – heavenly.

The triumph of the 4 x 4

"**Arrabal**" exposes the limits of the 2 x 4. It comes down to phrasing. D'Arienzo, don't forget, had rejected the 4 x 4 of De Caro, returning to the so-called 2 x 4 (really 4 x 8) of the *guardia vieja.* Láurenz, who had come out of the school of Julio De Caro and

[12] http://recordandotangos.blogspot.com/2009/05/la-musica-abre-puertas-que-nadie.html (accessed June 2012)

[13] María Suzana Azzi, Simon Collier: "Le Grand Tango: The Life and Music of Astor Piazzolla", OUP 2000, pp19-20

brought all those ideas with him, is having none of this. He sticks with the 4 x 4 but makes it dance music. This is an obvious thing to say, but 4 x 4 is twice as long as 2 x 4 which means it's much easier to make longer or more complex phrases. Láurenz takes full advantage. One of the most accomplished bandoneón virtuosos of all time, this piece is a showcase both of his musical vision and of his abilities on his instrument. Láurenz's final *variación* on the bandoneón is difficult to describe: not a breathtaking long phrase – you can hear that on "**Abandono**", which was recorded in the same session and appears on the other side of the disc – but a sequence of exuberant, joyful outpourings of unequalled creativity. The notes are tossed out like bouquets of flowers. There's nothing else like it in the canon: it's as if there is too much music in the man bursting to get out.

All this is in the music, but it's all about interpretation. Let's say, tango music is 90% composition – and 90% interpretation! We saw that with the Vardaro "**Tigre Viejo**" – his version has infinitely more punch than Fresedo's. It's the same with the creations of Julio De Caro's sextet, which were lovingly transformed by Osvaldo Pugliese into dance masterpieces. "**Arrabal**" is the direct descendent of the Vardaro "**Tigre Viejo**". This time the arrangement is not so much a work of transformation because the work appeared within the daring conception of the Vardaro sextet. Let's observe however that the only other orchestra to record "**Arrabal**" was fellow innovator Pugliese. All the other dance orchestras – Troilo, D'Arienzo, Di Sarli – didn't include it in their repertoire. Nor did the innovators of the early 1950s such as Salgán, Gobbi and Francini-Pontier. The work would simply not be attempted again until 1955, when Piazzolla arranged it for his octet. Piazzolla writes that it had seemed very innovative at the time, but it doesn't have the energy of the Láurenz version.

Pedro Láurenz also has a wonderful pianist possessed of excellent touch and timing. One wonders whether it might even have been Vardaro's pianist José Pascual, but it turns out that it wasn't: the pianist is the otherwise unknown Héctor Grané. It just goes to show the depth of the musical scene at this time. Grané's playing can be heard to good effect everywhere, but shines especially brilliantly in the valses where he is the foundation of the rhythmic drive of the orchestra.

We talk about Troilo's "**Milongueando en el '40**" being the manifesto of the 1940s but three years earlier it's all here in this incredible performance. Láurenz is truly ahead of his time.

Láurenz – a prodigy of the bandoneón

Maybe we should make a list of the top-ten *variaciones* in tango music (the *variación* is the twiddly bit that normally comes at the end of the song). If we did, Pedro Láurenz would fill more than half the places. Juan D'Arienzo has a fantastic bandoneón *section*, but the outstanding player of the day is Láurenz. His recordings contain a series of dazzling *variaciones* which leave one amazed. Many bandoneón players would play the bandoneón in only one direction, outwards, opening the bellows, and then take advantage of a pause in the music to release the air valve and collapse the bellows again. The bandoneóns literally take a breath. This is something you can hear for instance in D'Arienzo's variations.

There are two reasons why bandoneón players do this. The first is that the bandoneón is *diatonic* or properly speaking *bisonic*: pressing the same button, you get a different note playing inwards (closing the bellows) compared to playing outwards (opening the bellows), which means one has to learn the keyboard all over again. Every player learns and uses these other fingerings to a certain extent, but there is another reason why they don't use them so much: it is much harder to get the same tonal quality playing inwards.

When we listen to the bandoneón variations of the Láurenz orchestra it sounds to me as if Láurenz is playing in both directions, because the phrases are simply too long to be played with the breaths we mentioned above. This creates a sense of breathlessness in the listener which is tremendously exciting.

We already mentioned the B side of Arrabal, "**Abandono**", but a track I like even more is "**No me extraña**" (1940). I find it really hard to say why – both have great arrangements and fantastic *variaciones.* The music of the Láurenz orchestra is so packed with ideas and energy, it feels a bit like a runaway train that is just staying on the rails – something that we said about the Vardaro sextet, except this time it's a whole orchestra. "**No me extraña**" is just a tiny bit more measured. Maybe there is only so much wildness I can cope with, but I like to think that it's the combination of wildness with restraint that makes this so appealing.

Láurenz is also an outstanding interpreter of the vals, although it's hard to tell from the available transfers – "**Caserón de tejas**" has a barely adequate transfer whilst "**Flores del alma**" has never been reprinted at all. Console yourselves by listening to "**Mascarita**", once again full of excitement and invention. The milongas also have great drive: try "**La vida es una milonga**", with its hypnotic bandoneón riff from the very beginning of the piece and a joyful final variación in the piano.

The arrival of Alberto Podestá

Listen to the music and you'll hear that it falls neatly into two halves: before the arrival of singer Alberto Podestá at the beginning of 1943, and after. The incorporation of Podestá is a bit of a coup for Láurenz, as Podestá is very successful with Di Sarli at this time and moving to Láurenz would have been a step down financially. Their first recording together in April 1943, the sublime "**Nunca tuvo novio**" forms a bridge between the two periods. In this tango we can hear why Podestá has chosen to join Láurenz: the orchestra's daring conception and choice of material gives his voice room to soar and fly. It's a great performance, one of the orchestra's best.

In their second recording session, three months later, the music has developed so far that it almost sounds like another orchestra. "**Alma de bohemio**" is a masterpiece, and a watershed recording in tango music. When Podestá appears – at the usual place, one minute into the piece – he takes the lyric and immediately flies into the ether, holding a note for more than 10 seconds whilst the orchestra first of all comps[14] and then falls silent.

It would be four years before anyone else dares to follow suit: in 1947, D'Agostino tries the same thing. This is the Láurenz orchestra: consistently daring, consistently taking risks musically, always ahead of his time, and not making compromises with what will be commercial. This is wonderful dance music, just the thing when you want not just drive, but intelligence and daring.

The career of the Láurenz orchestra

After all this lavish praise, you are probably thinking that the career of the Láurenz orchestra is a catalogue of success. The discography tells a different story. In 1937, Láurenz recorded two 78s. In 1938, he recorded only one, and in 1939, none at all. Láurenz is not very commercially minded, and the wider public and more importantly the record companies just aren't ready. Success has to wait until 1940, but even then he is not prolific, recording only 28 records – 56 tracks – between their appearance in 1937 until the end of 1944, at which point Láurenz ceases to record for a while. When you consider how many pieces a working *orquesta típica* would have had in its repertoire (50? 100?), we can only imagine what riches went unrecorded, remembered only by those who heard them play.

These reflections remind me of one reason why I like analogue recordings more than digital ones. In the old acoustic system, it was the vibrations of the air itself, introduced by the musicians, which drove the stylus which then in turn cut the wax master. Think

[14] 'comping' is a shorthand in jazz for accompanying. It implies a simple regular accompaniment which supports a solo instrument.

about it: the sound directly created the recording, with no intermediary and no processing. The musicians vibrated the air which cut the record.

When electrical recording was introduced, this directness remained. There was still an immediate path from musician to record. It was literally a record of the music that was being played; that's why records are called records.

In the digital age, this is gone.

Pedro Láurenz on CD: what to listen to

Everything from Láurenz during this period is fantastic – and once again it's a history of infamy from the record companies, who incredibly – given that there are so few of them – have not released all of his recordings. Laúrenz's version of "**Flores del alma**" – perhaps the greatest recorded vals ever – has never been released on a commercial CD, whilst EMI themselves have not deigned to print "**Arrabal**", one of the most important tangos of all time. It's scandalous. Nevertheless, the real aficionados have managed to bring you at least some of this magisterial work. God bless you, Miguel Ángel Fernández (president of Euro Records).

The Euro album presents the earlier recordings and the 'Reliquias' CD the later ones. As we move into the mid 40s these have less pace, but the music is still finely crafted and danceable: "**Más solo que nunca**" with **Carlos Bermúdez** is a typical example, full of quality.

Euro	17015	Colección 78 RPM: Pedro Láurenz 1937/1943	2004
Reliquias	529110	Creaciones inolvidables con Podestá y Bermúdez	2000

Pedro Láurenz – discography (1937-1944)

1	14.07.37	Enamorado	Héctor Farrel	ranchera
2	14.07.37	Milonga de mis amores	Héctor Farrel	milonga
3	24.09.37	Arrabal		
4	24.09.37	Abandono	Héctor Farrel	
5	12.05.38	Vieja amiga	Juan Carlos Casas	
6	15.05.38	Milonga compadre	Juan Carlos Casas	milonga
7	25.01.40	No me extraña	Juan Carlos Casas	
8	25.01.40	De puro guapo	Juan Carlos Casas	
9	21.01.40	Mascarita	Juan Carlos Casas	vals
10	21.02.40	Desconsuelo	Juan Carlos Casas	
11	28.06.40	Milonga de mi flor	Juan Carlos Casas	milonga
12	28.06.40	Como dos extraños	Juan Carlos Casas	
13	29.07.40	Amurado	Juan Carlos Casas	
14	29.07.40	Improvisando	Juan Carlos Casas	milonga
15	05.09.41	La vida es una milonga	Martín Podestá	milonga
16	05.09.41	Orgullo criollo		
17	02.12.41	Quédate tranquil	Martín Podestá	
18	02.12.41	Poca suerte		
19	07.01.42	Al verla pasar	Martín Podestá	
20	07.01.42	Flores del alma	Martín Podestá	vals
21	31.03.42	Es mejor perdonar	Alberto Del Campo	
22	31.03.42	Caserón de tejas	Alberto Del Campo	vals
23	16.06.42	Corazón encadenado	Juan Carlos Casas	
24	16.06.42	Taconeando	Juan Carlos Casas	
25	20.10.42	A mí dejame en mi barrio	Juan Carlos Casas	
26	20.10.42	Chatero de aquel entonces	Juan Carlos Casas	milonga
27	02.12.42	Firuletear de bandoneón	Juan Carlos Casas	
28	02.12.42	María Remedios	Alberto Fuentes	vals
29	16.04.43	Nunca tuvo novio	Alberto Podestá	
30	16.04.43	Veinticuatro de agosto	Alberto Podestá	
31	15.07.43	Alma de bohemio	Alberto Podestá	
32	15.07.43	Patria mía	Alberto Podestá	
33	06.08.43	Garúa	Alberto Podestá	
34	06.08.43	Paisaje	Alberto Podestá	vals
35	22.09.43	Recién	Alberto Podestá	
36	22.09.43	Que nunca me falte	Alberto Podestá	
37	16.11.43	Yo quiero cantar un tango	Alberto Podestá	
38	16.11.43	Yo soy de San Telmo	Alberto Podestá	milonga
39	09.12.43	Todo	Alberto Podestá	
40	09.12.43	Maldonado	Alberto Podestá	milonga
41	14.01.44	Como el hornero	Alberto Podestá	
42	14.01.44	Milonga de mis amores		milonga
43	01.03.44	El criollito oriental	Alberto Podestá	milonga

44	01.03.44	Muchachos... mi último tango	Alberto Podestá	
45	26.04.44	Más solo que nunca	Carlos Bermúdez	
46	26.04.44	Llueve otra vez	Carlos Bermúdez	
47	26.04.44	Temblando	Carlos Bermúdez	vals
48	26.04.44	La madrugada	Carlos Bermúdez	
49	18.07.44	Naranjo en flor	Jorge Linares	
50	18.07.44	Corazón que me maltratas	Carlos Bermúdez	
51	07.08.44	Me están sobrando las penas	Carlos Bermúdez	
52	07.08.44	Esta noche al pasar	Jorge Linares	
53	04.10.44	Nada más que un corazón	Carlos Bermúdez	
54	04.10.44	Barrio tranquilo	Jorge Linares	
55	19.12.44	Trenzas	Jorge Linares	
56	19.12.44	Mendocina	Carlos Bermúdez; Jorge Linares	vals

14/ Roberto Firpo: the forgotten hero

Listening guide

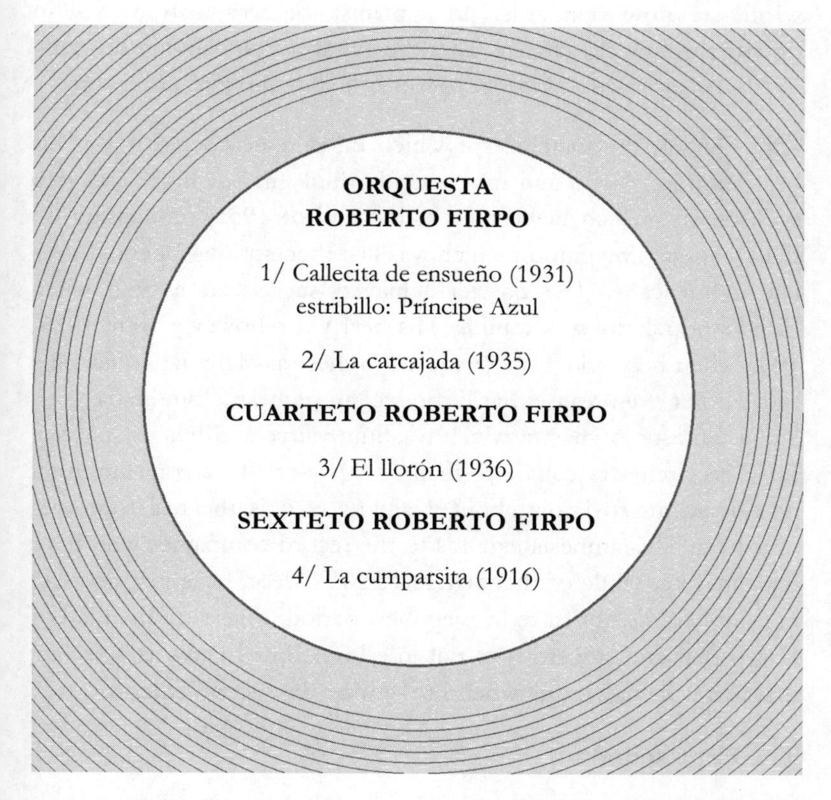

It is very difficult to find examples of Firpo's music that is commercially available. Please check the book's website www.tangomusicsecrets.com in case we've been able to update this list in the light of any new releases.

There were two great innovators in the 1920s, two orchestra leaders who were not only hugely influential but hugely successful as well. The first was Canaro, whom we spoke about earlier. He is certainly very well remembered even if the material that is most widespread today is not his best. The other was Roberto Firpo. Sad to say, he is now at best a marginalised figure amongst the modern tango public.

Firpo was an outstanding composer. So many of the songs he wrote are now standards. As a pianist, he was instrumental in driving through the change from the guitar to the piano in the early 1910s. As an orchestra leader however he has sunk into oblivion.

Like Canaro, the material for which he is remembered is not his best. Mention Firpo and most people think first of his *guardia vieja* style quartet which he formed at the end of 1935, capitalising on the D'Arienzo revolution which was just then striking Buenos Aires like a hurricane. The quartet achieved success at a time when Firpo's popularity was waning. His best years however were 1926-1935 when he worked only with his orchestra. Many tango dancers today don't even realise that Firpo had an orchestra, but he did – he had a fantastic orchestra which was innovative and hugely successful. This orchestra cut more than 2,000 sides! It's astonishing that no-one seems to know about it anymore. It is the real forgotten orchestra. This amnesia extends to the record companies who have reprinted very little of this material. EMI Odeón have just one CD in print and it's not from his very best period. These are the kind of claims that are dangerous to put in a book, but I can't help feeling that this will still be true when I'm writing the second edition.

The Firpo sound

The sound of the Firpo orchestra is distinctive – quite different to the tango that you are used to. For an introduction, let's listen to 1931's "**Callecita de ensueño**". The vocals are by Príncipe Azul – literally Prince Blue, which means something like Prince Charming. Although not from the top flight as a vocalist, he deserves our recognition as the man who coined D'Arienzo's nickname, *El rey del compás*.

The first thing to notice is the strong driving beat. I love the way Firpo treats the rhythm. Remember, Firpo had been instrumental in changing the guitar for the piano, and in then adding the double bass. These changes meant that the newly born *orquesta típica* had a whole new rhythmic engine that the trios and quartets of the first decade of the century had not possessed. In those early years of the 1910s Firpo had to keep the style of his piano playing fairly close to the guitar accompaniment in order to get the piano accepted, but once this was done he took full advantage of the new possibilities at his disposal, developing a rhythmic sound that is robust and yet soft at the same time. This is something that Canaro didn't really manage.

The next thing you'll notice is the sound of the violins, which are played slightly sharp and with such a deep vibrato that they almost wail. Firpo has a way of blending the different instruments together to create a wash of sound. The only other orchestra I can think of that does anything remotely similar is the later one of Carlos Di Sarli.

The tangos of Firpo's orchestra that are available on CD concentrate on the years 1935-1936, but I feel that this special combination of robustness and softness is at its most delicious in the years 1929-1931. Until 2011 these were the preserve of the collector and those willing to buy from Japan, but there are now two mp3 albums of this beautiful music.

When the D'Arienzo revolution hit in 1936 Firpo capitalised on the new-found popularity of the *guardia vieja* repertoire by founding a quartet to play in the old style. It proved very popular. Listen for instance to the bubbling backbeat in their knock-out recording of **"El llorón"** (1936).

The activities of this quartet didn't mean that Firpo gave up with his orchestra – he continued with both formats. The orchestra has  some great recordings: how about 1935's "**La carcajada**" ("The guffaw") in which the wailing violins imitate the sound of laughter. It seems that Canaro was not the only man unafraid to try out musical effects – musically speaking, Firpo's experiments were if anything even more successful.

Firpo the composer

In the 1910s, Firpo was a hugely important figure for the development of tango. Here are some of his innovative compositions – all of them standards of the modern repertoire, a century later.

1913: "**El amanecer**". Roberto Firpo's musical depiction of the dawn is said by some to have been inspired by Beethoven's Pastoral Symphony. I can't help noticing that this is the same time that Debussy was completing his second book of Preludes, called by some 'impressionist music'. This tango was a favourite of Carlos Di Sarli who recorded it three times. The exact year of composition is uncertain.

1914: "**Alma de bohemia**", a lyrical piece that sounds modern when it is picked up by Pedro Láurenz almost thirty years later. It was also recorded by Biagi, Pugliese, Tanturi and D'Agostino, as well as by the 1970s *guardia vieja* quartet Los Tubatango. Very few pieces have had such a broad appeal.

1920: "**Fuegos artificiales**" ("Fireworks"). Often cited as the first example of descriptive music in tango, this great composition really does depict the sound of a night of fireworks. Although later recorded by D'Arienzo and Troilo, Firpo is the only orchestra committed to maintaining the effect through the whole piece. His wailing violins really bring those rockets to life. Having listened to all three recordings whilst fireworks were going off outside, I prefer the second version (1928).

Other well-known compositions include: "**Argañaraz**" (most notably the recording by Tanturi), "**Viviani**" (Di Sarli, twice) and "**El rápido**" (Biagi, Rodríguez, Varela and memorably Piazzolla in 1947). Firpo also famously had a hand in the creation of "**La cumparsita**" which was brought to him in 1916 when it was still a march to see if he could arrange it into a tango. He could, and Firpo's quartet premiered the work that very night. He'd spend the rest of his life asking himself why he didn't put his name on the sheet music.

Firpo's 1916 recording of "**La cumparsita**" provides a real window into the past, as though the sound has taken a hundred years to travel down the horn of the gramophone. This is the first ever recording of the world's most famous tango and it is perhaps surprising how much of what we recognise today is already present. In particular, listen to the violin *obligato* – the wobbly violin solo that threads its way around the melody. This deep vibrato began to disappear with the later innovations of Julio De Caro, who gave violinists more interesting things to play.

Firpo the cattle rancher

No, really! In 1930, having made a fortune in tango and apparently at the peak of his creative powers, Firpo decided to become a cattle rancher. He bought a large hacienda in the countryside, investing most of his money in livestock. The first year everything went perfectly and Firpo made a million pesos. The following year most of his herd was killed by one of the regular floods of the Rio Paraná. Firpo invested the little he had left in the stock market where another crash wiped out his investment. There was nothing for it but to go back to work.

This is a great story but the discography shows a more nuanced view: Firpo spent only three months out of the studio during this cattle-ranching experiment, at the beginning of 1931.

Roberto Firpo: what to listen to

Orchestra:

CD	RGS	Tango Collection – Roberto Firpo	2011
mp3	DyM	tango classics 108: que te han hecho los muchachos	2011
mp3	DyM	tango classics 109: lo mismo que ayer	2011

Quartet:

CD	Reliquias	De la guardia vieja	1996

15/ Francisco Lomuto: firmly on the ground

Listening guide

ORQUESTA FRANCISCO LOMUTO

1/ Mano a mano (1936) estribillo: Jorge Omar

2/ Si soy así (1933) estribillo: Fernando Díaz

3/ Nunca más (1931)
estribillo: Alberto Acuña/Fernando Díaz

4/ Te aconsejo que me olvides (1928)

5/ Congojas que matan (v) (1931)
estribillo: Alberto Acuña/Fernando Díaz

6/ Lo que vieron tus ojos (v) (1933)
estribillo: Fernando Díaz/Mercedes Simone

7/ Parque Patricios (m) (1941)
canta: Fernando Díaz

How is it that an orchestra that recorded almost as many numbers as D'Arienzo is little mentioned nowadays? Maybe it's because Sony-BMG (who own RCA Victor) don't have a CD of his music in print. And why that might be is a mystery to me.

The Lomuto orchestra has a special and unique character. The band sounds like a weightier and more muscular version of Canaro, giving his music a heavier beat.

It turns out that Canaro and Lomuto were friends. When Lomuto was thinking of setting up on his own, he asked his friend if he could come into his orchestra to learn the ropes of running his own outfit. In effect, he apprenticed himself to Canaro who was thus his major influence musically. You can hear this quite clearly in the style of the arrangements and occasionally in the choice of repertoire.

Like Canaro, Lomuto experimented with adding different instruments to his line-up, but only a little. Again, like Canaro his music was not adventurous in the sense that tango historians mean it: it wasn't pushing any boundaries. Quite the opposite: Lomuto's music is conservative and it appealed to that section of society. His orchestra played at the Naval School and at La Casa del Gobierno – Government House itself. De Caro and Firpo may have played for high society; Lomuto played for the establishment.

The Lomuto orchestra hit its peak in the mid 1930s. We'll start with "**Mano a mano**", a track from 1936 which I feel was his very best year. This is the same time that Canaro was having his big hits with the singer Roberto Maida. It's immediately obvious that this is quite a different sound to its nearest neighbour. The beat has a heavy weight that comes from the left hand of the piano which comps along in synchrony with the double bass. The beat is good for walking and there's just enough going on elsewhere to keep it interesting. The lyrical interpretation of **Jorge Omar** gives the piece some air but you couldn't say that the piece flies – he is firmly pinned to the earth by the orchestra's elephant feet. It's the same with all the orchestra's hits from the same year: "**A la gran muñeca**", "**La cumparsita**" and an excellent version of "**Nostalgias**". You'll also hear that there is something very particular about the ending of all these tangos. Most tangos finish POM-POM, on a rising cadence (the first Pom is lower than the second one), but Lomuto goes the other way. Musicians tell us that this is a diminished seventh cadence and it gives the endings a unique feeling, very different to the other orchestras. This cadence is Lomuto's signature at the end of each tango.

Wind back the clock a few years to 1933 and the sound is a bit quicker but otherwise not really much different, for instance in the Lomuto classic "**Si soy así**"; and going back a couple of years further to 1931, "**Nunca más**" – another classic from this orchestra – things again don't seem any different. Do you remember that Canaro first experimented with a very strong beat around 1930-1932? The Lomuto sound of these years is now closer, but it doesn't seem to have developed very much thereafter.

Now Lomuto started recording as early as 1922, and if we go back into the late 1920s, a very special period in the history of tango, another side of his music emerges. This was the age of the sextets, and the tangos of the era had a slow and steady beat – qualities we very much associate with Lomuto. Does this mean that Lomuto's late 20s recordings are boring? Not at all – quite the opposite in fact. The music has more bounce. For instance, try 1928's "**Te aconsejo que me olvides**" which has a fantastic growling piano and plenty of dynamic. Lomuto has one more trick here. Do you remember D'Arienzo's *guardia vieja* ploy: simple violin solos played very low on the fourth string? Well Lomuto does the same thing, but at the other end of the fingerboard: simple violin solos but played very high on the first string.

The Lomuto repertoire

Lomuto championed a different repertoire to other orchestras. As with any good band there are tracks which we associate with him, but sometimes Lomuto's version is the only one. We've already mentioned a couple of tracks which fall into this category: "**Nunca más**", and "**Si soy así**". Without leafing through a discography, a couple more spring to mind: "**Dímelo al oído**" and "**Caminito**" – yes "Caminito", one of the most famous *tango-canciones!* We could also include "**Zorro gris**" – although this was picked up later by other orchestras, Lomuto's remains the only good interpretation by a dance orchestra of this *guardia vieja* theme. "**Nostalgias**" was also the only recording of that 1936 hit by a mainstream orchestra, although we can now appreciate the very fine version of a young Miguel Caló following its issue on CD by Euro Records.

Lomuto also brings his special qualities to the milonga and particularly to his valses which are truly delightful, perhaps because the light mood of the vals acts as a balance to the heavy weight of the Lomuto beat. An outstanding example would be "**Lo que vieron tus ojos**" (1933), sung *a dúo* with the famous female soloist **Mercedes Simone** guesting as the second voice – only Donato also attempted to mix male and female voices in this way. An even less common mood is established by "**Congojas que matan**" which features unusual harmonies in the voice with a wistful counter-melody in the very highest notes of the bandoneón.

Of Lomuto's milongas, his versions of "**No hay tierra como la mía**" (1939) and "**Parque Patricios**" (1941) are punchier (read: better) than Canaro's. There is also the unique "**Qué tiempo aquel**" (1938) in which Lomuto allows himself the use of drums, recalling his earlier forays into jazz. It really rocks!

What you should notice from these dates are, well, the dates! Although Lomuto recorded successfully well into the 1940s, his classic cuts are mostly from the 1930s. His is a *guardia vieja* orchestra. He was clever enough to survive into the 1940s but does not really contribute anything to the new wave of Di Sarli, Pugliese, Láurenz, Troilo and the others.

Back in the 1930s, however, his was a supremely important orchestra with unique qualities. This music establishes a special mood that is not as appreciated today as it might be by dancers, DJs and record companies alike: there are just three easily available CDs from an orchestra which cut nearly 1000 sides. Collectors will definitely be on the lookout for Japanese CDs with this orchestra. Some of the best late 1920s tracks can be now be heard on mp3 reissues.

Francisco Lomuto: what to listen to

CD	Euro	17001	Colección 78 RPM	2004
CD	Euro	17023	Colección 78 RPM 2 – 1931/1950	2005
CD	RGS	1715	Tango Collection	2011

European readers can buy the following mp3 album on iTunes, which appears to be a reissue of tracks across three deleted CDs of the 'el bandoneón' label.

mp3	Mundo Latino		The Roots of Tango – Nostalgias	2012

16/ Osvaldo Fresedo: sweet and lovely

Listening guide

SEXTETO
OSVALDO FRESEDO

1/ El once (1927)

ORQUESTA OSVALDO FRESEDO

2/ El once (1935) estribillo: Roberto Ray
3/ El once (1945)
4/ Vida mía (1933) estribillo: Roberto Ray
5/ Araca la caña (1933) estribillo: Roberto Ray
6/ Buscándote (1941) canta: Ricardo Ruíz
7/ Plegaria (1941) canta: Ricardo Ruíz

Here's what everyone normally says about Fresedo: sweet, romantic music, sometimes sugary sweet. Of course it's mostly true, and that was my first impression too.

We can get an overview of Fresedo's output very quickly by listening to three versions of the tango "**El once**", his own composition and one he recorded many times. The first version comes from his sextet period in 1927; the second, from 1935, belongs to Fresedo's golden years with his emblematic singer Roberto Ray whom it features on vocals; and the third, instrumental once again, comes from 1945.

The opening notes of the first two versions create a similar impression, which is a charming one. In comparison the 45 version sounds overblown: in the first five seconds we get drums, a big descending *glissando* on the piano, and a few chords on the vibraphone. Ouch.

When we listen to the first two versions more closely the differences emerge. Both belong firmly to the periods they were recorded in. Let's take a look.

Fresedo with Roberto Ray: a smooth combination

Fresedo's 1935 version of "**El once**" with Roberto Ray is a classic and it's typical of their output in this period. Ray's voice is refined, and Fresedo – Ray is a very smooth combination indeed. It might well remind us a little of Canaro's recordings with Maida.

Ray's slightly restrained voice perfectly suits the sophisticated, upper-class air of the orchestra; this is posh tango, straight out of the Palm Court at the Waldorf Hotel. It's the kind of tango that would have fitted a 1930s Hollywood movie just right. One can only wonder what a working man would have made of it back in the 1930s, but he wouldn't have had much opportunity to hear this music, other than on the radio: Fresedo was born into a wealthy family and the upper classes formed his clientele.

Now it may come as a surprise, but Ray joined the Fresedo orchestra as early as 1933, and was singing with him occasionally back in 1931. You'll remember that Canaro went through a few years in the early 1930s with a strong upbeat style before going to something softer with Roberto Maida in 1935. Fresedo makes a much smoother transition, and with hindsight it begins to feel that he may have influenced Canaro here, because Ray's 1933 tracks have all the quality and style of the later ones. The quality is consistently high – there just isn't a bad track, and the odd fox-trot or rumba are equally pleasing. Moreover the sound doesn't really change at all over those years (1933-39): the pace and mood of "**Vida mía**", recorded in September 1933, is very similar for instance to "**Ojos muertos**", recorded in November 1938. Only at the very edges can we hear anything different: the tracks from Ray's final session in January 1939 are a bit more sugary, prefiguring the 1940s period with Ricardo Ruíz and others, whilst Ray's very first recordings such as "**Araca la caña**" (June 1933) have a slightly faster pace.

Ray left the orchestra at the beginning of 1939, just as the shift to the *cantor de orquesta* is happening. After more than seven years with the orchestra he was probably in search of a new challenge, and he formed his own band in collaboration with the pianist and arranger José Rizzuti. They were successful on the radio but left no recordings.

This is a pity because Roberto Ray was a big influence on the development of tango. He was perhaps the first to sing tango with an orchestra without trying to identify himself as a man of the street. From him comes a line of development that passes through Roberto Maida and leads on to Francisco Fiorentino. Roberto Ray may not be the first *cantor de orquesta*, but he is the prototype.

Fresedo after Roberto Ray

Fresedo's style becomes more and more affected after Roberto Ray and our interest in the orchestra begins to decline. The recordings

with Ricardo Ruíz vary from the sublime ("**Buscándote**") to the

ridiculous ("**Plegaria**"). Fresedo chooses fine voices such as Carlos Mayel and notably **Oscar Serpa**, who went on to sing with Di Sarli. Serpa has a few fine tracks, although they are hard to find in good fidelity, but in general he cannot save the orchestra from the material.

1950 inaugurated a big change for Fresedo – as it did for many orchestras. Fresedo recruited Roberto Pansera as his arranger and he made sweeping changes, with some fast paced milongas and a few arrangements of Piazzolla numbers. Some of this is okay but it never reaches classic status.

Fresedo before Roberto Ray

Fresedo made his first recordings in 1922. What then was he doing just before Ray joined? It's not so easy to find out. Fresedo was signed to the defunct Brunswick label in the years 1930-1932 with whom he made 48 recordings. Although these have never been formally presented on CD, there are seven tracks hidden away on the CD 'Rendezvous Porteño' (which features some live recordings of the jazz trumpeter Dizzy Gillespie improvising with the orchestra during a visit to Buenos Aires in 1956), in addition to a few tracks made available by private collectors. Brunswick's Argentine ledgers have been lost (!) so we don't know the matrix numbers – Brunswick didn't print them on the labels – or exactly when within this period the recordings were made. All we can see are the disc numbers which enables us to place the music in rough chronological order.

Now we know that Canaro changed his style around 1930, abandoning the intimate music of the late 20s in favour of a hard and fast beat. We know too that Fresedo's first records with Ray on the Victor label in 1933 were more up-beat. Was he exploring the same vein then as Canaro in his Brunswick years?

It turns out that, no, he wasn't. The Brunswick recordings are quite similar to the sextet recordings from the late 1920s (more on those later) until the very last ones, when we can hear the beginnings of the romantic style. There's no increase in pace: Fresedo is not following Canaro here, and why should he, since he was just as successful at the time.

Is it then a smooth transition from the Brunswick recordings to the Victor ones with Roberto Ray? Not quite. There's one big difference. Fresedo has switched from the sextet to the orchestra, and this allows him to increase the sophistication of his orchestrations. This change is integrated very swiftly in musical terms, just a few months.

The Osvaldo Fresedo sextet

What about Osvaldo Fresedo's sextet? I'm itching to tell you all about it, but that must wait until we talk about it in-depth in chapter 19, the era of the sextets. For now, let's listen to the sextet recording of "**El once**" from 1927. This is Fresedo with a romantic sensibility but stripped of the sugary adornments which would later overwhelm his music: it's Fresedo unplugged. I love it.

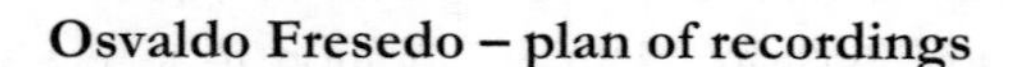

Osvaldo Fresedo – plan of recordings

- 1922 - 1926: acoustic recordings (sextet)
- 1926 - 1928: sextet recordings on Victor
- 1930 - 1932: sextet recordings on Brunswick, most with *estribillista*
- 1933 - 1939: orchestra recordings with Roberto Ray
- 1939 - 1941: Ricardo Ruíz & Carlos Mayel
- 1942 - 1946: Oscar Serpa

From the discussion above, our interest in the orchestra is going to focus on the years 1926-1942: not so different from many of the other orchestras.

Fresedo on CD: what to listen to

We start with Roberto Ray, pick up the best of the later work and then grab the 'Tango Collection' CD to listen to the sextet recordings.

TARG	41287	Tangos de salon	1996
Euro	17048	Colección 78 RPM: Tigre Viejo 1933/1948	2009
Euro	17034	Colección 78 RPM 2: Osvaldo Fresedo 1933/1948	2005
Euro	17013	Colección 78 RPM: Osvaldo Fresedo 1938/1948	2004
RGS	1643	Tango Collection – Osvaldo Fresedo	2012

For the curious, the Acqua records CD 'Rendezvous Porteño' is worth listening to for the sextet recordings made on Brunswick around 1931-1932, although the sound fidelity is not great.

17 / Alfredo De Angelis & the two tenors

Listening guide

ORQUESTA
ALFREDO DE ANGELIS

1/ Marioneta (1943) canta: Floreal Ruíz

2/ De igual a igual (1944)
canta: Julio Martel, glosa Nestor Rodi

3/ La cumparsita (1944) glosa Nestor Rodi

4/ Pregonera (1945) cantan: Dante - Martel

5/ Soñar y nada más (v) (1944) cantan: Dante - Martel

6/ Soy un arlequín (1944) canta: Carlos Dante

7/ Va llegando gente al baile (1944)
canta: Julio Martel

Alfredo De Angelis had a tango orchestra which made music for dancers that was light and romantic. You may feel that the term "light romantic music" is not always a compliment, and you would be right: Alfredo De Angelis's music was not universally liked. His detractors called it *música de calesita* – merry-go-round music – but we shouldn't take them too seriously. Doubtless they were some of the same people who didn't like D'Arienzo.

De Angelis arrived on the scene a little late, forming his orchestra in 1941 and only making his first recordings in 1943. By this time every orchestra which could afford it had two singers. Whom did De Angelis choose? Well, the first choice was the young and relatively unknown **Julio Martel.** Today we don't really remember any of Martel's solo recordings as classics. To get an idea of his voice let's listen to "**De igual a igual**" which has a dramatic spoken introduction or *glosa.* If the voice which then sings sounds different to the one which reads the introduction, well, it is. Back in the day, every band would have their own announcer, someone chosen for their dramatic delivery. He would be the one chosen to read the *glosas.* I say read, but the *glosa* is poetry and as such it would be not so much read as declaimed.

Not many *glosas* made it onto disc: the most famous example is Angel D'Agostino's "**Café Dominguez**", which has only a *glosa* and no lyric. De Angelis's *glosas* were read by his announcer Nestor Rodi who recorded quite a few, including a unique early version of "**La cumparsita**" which has Rodi going into a frenzy and then handing over perfectly to the bandoneóns.

It took De Angelis a year to find the right partner for Martel. For the first year the second singer was the very fine **Floreál Ruíz**. Listening to their recordings such as "**Marioneta**" the combination works very well indeed. Maybe Ruíz felt he could do better – he would later sing for Troilo, the dream orchestra for any singer. Perhaps he was just too good for De Angelis. For whatever reason he moved on and his replacement was **Carlos Dante**.

Now, Dante was not really an obvious choice for a young orchestra because he was a veteran of the old guard. He had toured in Spain with Rafael Canaro (one of Francisco's Canaro's brothers) around 1929-1930. He'd also sung and recorded with a young Miguel Caló in the years 1934-1936. After all these successes he was tired of the bohemian life and was on the verge of retirement. He had taken a job with an oil company and was singing in his spare time for a minor orchestra. De Angelis persuaded him to come out of retirement and paired him with Julio Martel, thus combining youth with experience.

The innovation of De Angelis arose simply from how well these two voices went together. It was normal for bands to perform the occasional duet with both their singers – we have recorded examples from all the Big Four orchestras. De Angelis quickly realised that his two voices blended together exceptionally well. Martel's voice (not actually a tenor, but a baritone) was richer and had more body; Dante's could soar more. Although both were very good, neither was at the level of a Francisco Fiorentino or a Roberto Chanel, but together – with Martel's baritone given the lower voice and Dante's tenor the higher – De Angelis had a match-winning combination. It was a hit and the public loved it.

Listen to the tango "**Pregonera**", the second duet they recorded together, and listen to how De Angelis combines the voices. The voices alternate for the verse (quiz question: which enters first?) and then combine for the chorus. It's just delightful, even more so

in the valses which really soar. "**Soñar y nada más**" is a lovely example, surpassing the interpretation of its composer, Francisco Canaro.

Not just a double act

The beauty of the duets shouldn't prevent us from appreciating the numbers that these two recorded individually. I'd suggest starting

with Carlos Dante and his tango "**Soy un arlequín**" (1945). Dante has great phrasing and suits the light feel of the orchestra. Martel solo is not quite as satisfying: only his early tracks with the orchestra such as "Va llegando gente al baile" (1944) have enduring appeal.

These two vocalists take us right through the 1940s. Martel left to go solo in 1951, apparently with tears in his eyes at his final performance. De Angelis replaced him with the powerful voice of **Oscar Larroca** and again pushed the duets. Commercially he was successful, maintaining his orchestra until 1991 – a real achievement – but with the odd exception the best of the music is naturally to be found in the 1940s recordings.

De Angelis on CD: what to listen to

The De Angelis orchestra stayed with EMI-Odeón until 1977 and cut their final album as late as 1985.

EMI have reissued two thirds of the 486 recordings that De Angelis made with them; some may feel, given the thin quality of some of the later material, that this is rather too many. Concentrate on the earlier recordings. The 'From Argentina to the World' CD is a good way to pick up the unique late instrumental "**Pavadita**" without having to wade through less interesting material.

Of the CDs featuring Carlos Dante, the best one is '20 Exitos vol.1 canta Carlos Dante' which contains the wonderful tango "**Gloria**".

Reliquias	499993	Los dúos de Carlos Dante y Julio Martel	1999
EMI	371954	From Argentina to the World	1996
Reliquias	529106	Ruíz-Martel-Dante: sus primeros vocalistas	2000
Reliquias	595166	Los Primeros Instrumentales	2003
Reliquias	473889	20 Exitos vol.1 canta Carlos Dante	2004

18/ Lucio Demare: tango italiano

Listening guide

1/ Roberto Murolo: Nemica

ORQUESTA LUCIO DEMARE

1/ Malena (1942)
canta: Juan Carlos Miranda

2/ Tal vez sera su voz (1943)
canta: Raúl Berón

3/ Solamente… ella (1944)
canta: Horacio Quintana

4/ Igual que un bandoneón (1945)
canta: Horacio Quintana

If there was ever an orchestra that displayed the influence of Neapolitan song on tango – then it was the one led by Lucio Demare.

Now I'm being a bit disingenuous here. Or am I? Neapolitan song sounds nothing like tango music, does it?

The greatest exponent of Neapolitan song was the Naples born Roberto Murolo (1912-2003) who recorded extensively over his long career. Listen for instance to "**Nemica**", which was the first song that came up when I searched for him on-line, and tell me if it couldn't be arranged as a tango. Then listen to the style of singing – it's very lyrical. Now, lyricism is exactly the ingredient that distinguishes the tangos of the 40s from those of the 20s. Italians were the single largest ethnic group in Argentina, and they emigrated from the ports: in the north, Genoa, and in the south – Naples, particularly in the inter-war period, which is exactly the period we are interested in. Argentine Spanish is basically Spanish with an Italian accent, and research suggests that the *porteño* intonation most closely resembles that of Naples.

This lyricism reaches its peak in the lush combination of Lucio Demare with his best singer Juan Carlos Miranda. Their greatest track has to be the iconic "**Malena**" (1942), the music for which was written in a café by Demare himself in under fifteen minutes.

After Miranda came **Raúl Berón** who joined Demare from the orchestra of Miguel Caló. They did record some nice tracks – listen for instance to "**Tal vez sera su voz**" (1943) – but at other times Berón's voice sounds too light for Demare's rich strings. I wish he'd stayed with Caló.

Berón lasted only a year and his replacement **Horacio Quintana** suits the orchestra much better. His voice is reminiscent of Miranda, although it's not as rich. "**Solamente… ella**" (1944) is an exquisite although perhaps atypical example of their work. For a more typical tango, listen to "**Igual que un bandoneón**" (1945). This beautiful rendition is certainly the equal of the version of Tanturi with Campos.

Lucio Demare on CD: what to listen to

Demare was very successful but not very commercially minded, meaning than he cut less than a hundred sides when he could have made many more.

Start with the recordings with Miranda, and watch out for the fact that he recorded "**Malena**" twice – the second performance dates from 1951 and like so many vocal performances from the 50s is not very satisfying.

To pick up the superb 1938 milonga "**La esquina**" you have to buy the CD 'Tres Orquestas Milongueras' on Euro Records' imprint 'Archivo Odeón'.

Finally there is an album of Demare's solo piano work, originally recorded in 1968 and released as an LP. Demare's solo piano work can sound quite wistful; it's a very different feeling to his orchestral work. The CD version of this album is out-of-print. However to hear Demare as a soloist, I far prefer listening to the **Trio Argentino** in which Lucio Demare accompanied Canaro's two early singers Agustín Irusta and Roberto Fugazot. There is a CD with good fidelity on RGS's 'Tango Collection'.

Reliquias	529132	Sus éxitos con Miranda, Berón y Quintana	2000
Reliquias	541698	Sus primeros éxitos	2002
Reliquias	499978	Sus éxitos con Raúl Berón	1999
Euro	19012	Tres Orquestas Milongueras: Lucio Demare - Miguel Caló - Pedro Láurenz	2007
RGS	1692	Tango Collection : Trio Argentino	1994

Part 3

The roaring twenties

The Golden Decade in context

So far in the book we've explored the orchestras of the Golden Decade and we also touched on the years leading up to it. Let's sum up what we've learnt about the developments of the 1930s. In those years there are two trends in tango music. First of all there is the traditional mainstream: Canaro, Lomuto, Firpo, each pursuing their own styles within the overall space of tango music which is evolving organically. The big names survive into the 40s but fade in importance.

Slightly more adventurous are the romantics, Fresedo and Di Sarli. Fresedo is doing well in the mid 30s but Di Sarli has temporarily disappeared from the scene. He will return to be a major force in the Golden Decade.

Finally there is a more innovative group, a smaller group of musicians who are seeking to push the boundaries of tango. For this group their time has not yet come. Some of them – Láurenz, Pugliese – are from the school of De Caro, but others – Vardaro, José Pascual – are not. We can trace this trend right back to the Vardaro-Pugliese sextet of 1930. It's hard to say when this trend ripens because the record companies aren't recording this music, which they consider non-commercial. If this frustrates us today, we can only imagine how people must have felt at the time. On the evidence that we have, the music matures in 1937 with Láurenz's "Arrabal".

But we can say when the public were ready to accept it. That would be at the end of 1938, with the change from the estribillista to the *cantor de orquesta*, the orchestra singer.

The Golden Decade is not the only decade

Argentines place most emphasis on what they call the "Golden Decade of the 1940s" for socio-historical reasons: this is when the tango nightlife of Buenos Aires was at its most intense, and its famous Calle Corrientes (Corrientes Street) was earning its reputation as the "street which never sleeps". As dancers we've already seen that our emphasis is slightly earlier, our own Golden Decade being the years 1935-1944. Even so, it's easy to end up with the impression that this was the "best" period of tango, with everything that happened before this time just serving to lead up to it.

D'Arienzo was the most successful artist of the Golden Decade, but does that mean he was the most successful artist overall? We've already hinted that things may not be so simple. We don't have sales figures but we do know roughly how many recordings each group made. So, how prolific were the different orchestras? To gauge our own ideas about the importance and success of the different orchestras, I invite you to arrange the following list in order, paying special attention to the Big Four. Answers overleaf.

- Biagi
- Caló
- Canaro
- D'Arienzo
- De Angelis
- De Caro
- Di Sarli
- Donato
- Firpo
- Fresedo
- Lomuto
- Orquesta Típica Victor (OTV)
- Pugliese
- Rodríguez
- Troilo

Recorded output of the main tango orchestras

1/ Canaro: 3,798
2/ Firpo: 2,862
3/ Fresedo: 1,252
4/ D'Arienzo: 963 + 43* = 1006
5/ Lomuto: 958
6/ Juan Maglio: c. 900
7/ De Angelis: 551
8/ Pugliese: 473
9/ Troilo: 454 + 34 = 488
10/ OTV: 446
11/ De Caro: 417
12/ Caló: 384
13/ Donato: 355
14/ Di Sarli: 326 + 49 = 375
15/ Rodríguez: 354
16/ Biagi: 187

How did you do? Not very well, I suspect, since of our Big Four orchestras only D'Arienzo makes it into the top four places – and Canaro beats him by almost four to one. What's going on?! When did Canaro make all these recordings? Certainly not in the 40s, when D'Arienzo was selling more records than anyone.

The answer is that there is a lot more to tango than the Golden Decade of the 1940s. Canaro, Firpo, Fresedo and Lomuto had a huge output earlier, in the 1920s and early 1930s. It's time to learn more about that era, an important one not just for historians, but for dancers too.

---

* The smaller number is the number of the sextet recordings for D'Arienzo and Di Sarli, and the number of quartet recordings for Troilo. Not all of D'Arienzo's recordings were under his sole name: some were made as the D'Arienzo-Visca sextet.

19 / The era of the sextets

Listening guide

Francisco Lomuto:
Te aconsejo que me olvides (1928)

Osvaldo Fresedo: Tinta verde (1928)
La cachila (1927)

Francisco Canaro: Derecho viejo (1928)

Carlos Di Sarli: No te aguanto más (1929)

Julio De Caro: El taita (Raza criolla) (1928)

Pedro Maffia: Un pobre borracho (1929)

Juan Guido: Gusanito (1927)

The era I want to tell you about now is not really the twenties, but a very special period just at the end of the 1920s when the early sextets – two bandoneóns, two violins, piano and double bass – were making fabulous music that we still enjoy today. We can pin it down pretty precisely to the couple of years beginning in November 1926.

The tango group had evolved in a short time from an early trio of guitar, flute and violin to a sextet of piano, double bass, two violins and two bandoneóns, with Canaro and Firpo leading the way. Then something very special happened: electrical recording was invented. Why was this important? How were recordings made previously?

Before the advent of electrical recording, discs were recorded acoustically. The mechanism was very much like an old gramophone, but operating in reverse. The musicians huddled together around an enlarged horn which transmitted the sound to a stylus which in turn cut the groove into a wax disc.

The problems of this system were mainly down to the horn, which was necessary to collect sound and focus it onto the cutting stylus. The sound that made it to onto the disc was the sound that made it to the end of the horn, which is another way of saying that it was rather like listening to the band by holding a horn to your ear. The effect is a bit like going to the opera but then listening to the performance not in the auditorium, but from down the end of a corridor. The music sounds distant and muted because the very low and very high notes just don't make it down the horn.

This process was revolutionized by new technology that came out of Bell Laboratories in the United States in 1924. The real innovation was the new-fangled vacuum tube or valve which made it possible to make use of the condenser microphone. This had been invented a few years earlier and had a good frequency response. The trouble was that it didn't produce a big enough signal by itself to cut a record.

Using valves, the engineers at Bell Laboratories created the very first amplifier. This solved the problem of the microphone's quiet signal. For recording purposes, but not for playback, the horn was eliminated, meaning that the recordings no longer sounded distant. The results were a vast improvement on what had gone before.

The new technology arrived in Argentina at the end of 1925 but bizarrely it was not introduced for almost a year. The problem was that the record companies had huge stocks of acoustic discs, and if they trumpeted the benefits of the new electrical system, the public might not buy them.

Odeón and Victor came to a gentlemen's agreement and the new technology was slipped in quietly at the end of 1926, unannounced save for the presence of the letter "e" before the number of the disc. Odeón made their first recordings with the new technology on 8th November, 1926. Matrices #4 and #5 were recorded by Firpo, but of more interest to us are the next three, #6, #7 and #8, which were given to Francisco Canaro. Curiously, both of them recorded the tango "**Anoche a los dos**", but the work that has been remembered was Canaro's other side, "**A media luz**". We listened to it earlier when we discussed Canaro. All these years later, both the fidelity of the sound and the quality of the music still sound remarkably good.

Of course, none of this would be of any interest if the music wasn't worth listening to. The sextets of Fresedo and Lomuto were recording as early as 1922, and Canaro's even earlier, but the music sounds boring. What had happened in the meantime?

1926: Electrical recording arrives in Argentina

Looking in the Odeón register, matrices #4 and #5 went to Firpo #,6, #7 and #8 went to Canaro. What about the first three matrices?

Odeón gave these to Carlos Gardel who was actually signed to Victor. Gardel already had experience of electrical recordings – he'd made some in Barcelona a year earlier. He wasn't happy with the sound of these first recordings and so they were never published. He continued to record for a while longer using the old acoustic system, until he was completely satisfied with the new technology.

These first recordings were made at 80rpm. It was only in 1927 that Odeón standardised at 78prm. That's just two months (November and December 1926) at 80rpm but in this time Canaro recorded 12 numbers and Firpo 47.

You'll sometimes hear talk about how in the early days of recording the speed was not well controlled. Early gramophones had a lever to control the playback speed, and the listener adjusted this until the music sounded right – perhaps the same as what he had heard in a live performance or on the radio.

All this is true but it happened well before the years of electrical recording. All tango recordings made at 78rpm were made at precisely that speed. The only confusion comes from a trick used by the record companies in the golden decade: they deliberately cut the master at a slower speed (Odeón are said to have used 76 RPM) so that when the disc was played back at 78 RPM the music sounded faster and brighter. The bands sometimes tried to compensate by playing more slowly for recording sessions but the change in pitch was unavoidable: bandoneóns cannot be re-tuned.

The influence of Julio De Caro

The answer is that Julio De Caro had happened. Declaring that "tango is also music" he allowed himself to think outside the box, introducing harmonic richness into all the instruments. Today all of his musicians are remembered for their individual contributions: his brother Francisco for his rich piano playing, Julio himself for his violin, and, especially, the dazzling virtuosity of his two bandoneón players, Pedro Láurenz and Pedro Maffia, for instance in their 1928 recording of "**El taita (Raza criolla)**", recorded by Pugliese in 1945. The De Caro performance has none of the passion and drive of Pugliese's later interpretations but the arrangement is almost identical. De Caro sends the melody around his group in the manner of a symphony orchestra performing Tchaikovsky.

The music

The most accessible of the sextets is undoubtedly Canaro. His sextet recordings are, as we noted earlier, already very developed musically, and there are many stylistic elements that we can recognise in his later work, for instance the style of the bandoneón arrangements. We've already listened to works of tremendous musical invention such as "**Derecho viejo**" (1927).

Nevertheless, if I could choose only one of these sextets for you to listen to, it would be that of Osvaldo Fresedo. This is a Fresedo that is largely unrecognisable from the orchestra that we are familiar with. The music is sophisticated but without the polish that we so think of as core to the Fresedo sound. The arrangements, whilst spacious, have meat and bite, at times veritably prowling as for instance in "**La cachila**" (1927). This is an unusual and daring composition but it is also given a daring arrangement. Canaro, who recorded everything – over 300 numbers in 1927 alone – never attempted it.

Another largely neglected sextet is that of Francisco Lomuto. There are no fireworks but his walking beat in tracks such as "**Te aconsejo que me olvides**" (1928) is irresistible. This makes quite a contrast to the immortal Troilo-Fiorentino version of 1941.

Lomuto's sextet version of "**Cuando llora la milonga**" (1930) meanwhile has some great violin *obligato*, nice syncopation and even features a final solo on the oboe, all tricks we associate more with his mentor Francisco Canaro.

Then there are the groups that really belong to this period alone such as those of Francisco Pracánico or **Juan Bautista Guido**. His 1927 tango "**Gusanito**" can't match Fresedo or Canaro in the richness of its arrangement but it is very playful. If better transfers were available I am sure we would be listening to him more.

Silent pictures, talking pictures

Back in the 1920s there was no television – that was still some way off. Radio broadcasts had begun in 1920 but the average person couldn't afford a set. For most people, the only way to hear music was to hear it played live.

Now for this, what do you think your options were? If you were rich, you could attend a private party, or organise one yourself. If you weren't, you would have to go to a venue where the band was playing. These were cafés but also – wait for it – cinemas! This was the era of silent movies, and tango bands used to play during the performances. If you think how big cinema was in the pre-TV era then it's easy to see that this was a huge source of employment for musicians.

Today we imagine that silent films had special scores written for them, to go with the action in the film. This was true for many of the big films, especially towards the end of that era, but often the bands would improvise or just play whatever they liked. Argentine bands liked playing tango music, so going to the cinema was a great way to hear it. It's said that people went to the cinema as much to listen to tango music as to watch the film.

Then in 1931, talking pictures arrived in Argentina. The cinemas installed the new sound equipment and this lucrative source of work dried up overnight. At the same time, the smaller record labels went bust whilst the larger ones cancelled the contracts of their less lucrative artists. It was a calamity. The biggest orchestras survived: Canaro, Fresedo, Lomuto and Firpo, but elsewhere many tango musicians found themselves out of work. Carlos Di Sarli lost his recording contract and was reduced to odd-jobbing as a backing musician for Mercedes Carné.

The biggest loss from our point of view was **Pedro Maffia**. He was famous for the dark, velvety tone of his bandoneón which you can hear for instance on "**Un pobre borracho**" (1929). This is a typical Maffia arrangement – nuanced, rich and unhurried. The violin *obligato* part sounds a bit different: Maffia has handed it to – can you guess? It's a cello.

By the time Maffia made a comeback, in 1934, tango music had become stronger, coarser even. These changes didn't suit him. When the tidal wave generated by the explosion of Juan D'Arienzo swept across the musical landscape, he decided it was too late for his subtle style and quietly retired, leaving no further recordings.

The sextets on CD: what to listen to

CD	DyM	3008	Que bonboncito	2002
CD	DyM	3401	Pedro Maffia	2003
CD	RGS	1641	Tango Collection – Julio De Caro	2011
CD	RGS	1643	Tango Collection – Osvaldo Fresedo	2012
CD	RGS	1653	Tango Collection – Carlos Di Sarli 1928-1931	2011
CD	RGS	1715	Tango Collection – Lomuto	2011

For Francisco Canaro there is unbelievably nothing in print from this period, which includes much of his best work.

20/ Julio De Caro:

tango is music

El tango también es música

Tango is also music

– Julio De Caro

Listening guide

SEXTETO
JULIO DE CARO

1/ Flores negras (1927)

ORQUESTA JULIO DE CARO

2/ Taba calzada (1935)

3/ Saca chispas (m) (1938)

4/Catamaraca (1940)

5/ Sopresa de novia (v) 1943

6/ Mi dolor (1950)
canta: Orlando Verri

7/ Flores negras (1952)

Any mention of Julio De Caro usually begins with a discussion of the contributions he made to the musical possibilities within tango. Indeed, we said some of the very same things ourselves in the previous chapter. However, I'd like to start by posing a question that is rather more basic for the tango dancer. Is the orchestra of Julio De Caro a dance orchestra?

Keep this in mind as we go on.

Julio De Caro was born into a rich family which no doubt was proud of the musical abilities and education of its children: Julio and Emilio on violin, and Francisco on piano. His father José had taught in the conservatoire at La Scala in Milan and had established a music shop and school in Buenos Aires. All the children were given a musical education but the father's hope was that Julio would study medicine, or at least become first violin in a symphony orchestra.

The story goes that Vicente Greco, an influential composer and bandleader at that time, was a frequent visitor. On one occasion when Julio was just nine years old his violin lesson was interrupted by one of these visits. At that time (1910) all Buenos Aires was agog at the state visit of Isabella, the "Infanta", a term used in Spain to designate members of the royal family who were not first in line to the throne. Greco had written a tango in her honour, "La Infanta" and had come round to play it. De Caro wrote[15]:

> *Eager to express my admiration, I grabbed my violin and began to play his tango "El pibe", for which I had the sheet music, and had learnt without my father's knowledge. Such an attitude was not welcomed by the latter but I managed to hear Greco say: "This kid will go far with his vocation. Who says he's not going to be a tango master?". But he answered: "Never, I have planned a different destiny for Julio!"*

---

[15] quoted by Juan Silbido in "Evocación del Tango", Buenos Aires, 1964

Julio was put on bread and water for eight days but was not to be deterred. As he grew up he started to visit tango venues. On one occasion when Julio was seventeen years old he went to hear Firpo play at the Palais de Glace. At one point in the evening, which we can only presume was quite animated, his friends forced him up onto the stage. The violin player gave up his instrument and De Caro played a tango to wild applause.

It just so happened that Eduardo Arolas ("the tiger of the bandoneón") was present in the audience. He was so impressed that a few days later he visited Julio's father to ask whether Julio could join his orchestra.

As you'll have guessed, the answer was no but once he reached eighteen he joined the group of Ricardo Brignolo (author of the tango "**Chiqué**"). When his father found out, Julio was thrown out of the house. At this his brother Francisco decided not to wait to be asked, and left as well. You and I have great reason to be grateful that they both made this fateful choice because it hugely enriched our music and influenced many of the musicians that we love today, most famously Osvaldo Pugliese.

This is a long time before the De Caro sextet appeared in 1924. We could regale you with tales of the brothers' musical adventures in the meantime, but I want to tell you the story of how the sextet was born. In fact, it was Francisco De Caro and not Julio who put the sextet together. This is how it happened: in December 1923 an impresario asked Francisco to put together a group of five or six musicians to play at New Year's parties in high society mansions. The fee offered was the fantastic amount of 800 pesos per musician – a month's pay. Francisco called together his brothers Julio and Emilio on violin, Pedro Maffia and Luis Petrucelli on bandoneón, and Leopoldo Thompson, the emblematic bass player of the period. In evening dress and impeccably behaved, things went off brilliantly. The brothers were finally together.

The group got work in a café, the Café Colón. It was not very well paid but they managed to get a contract for the carnival season, for which the brothers expanded the line-up to 20 musicians under Julio's name. Returning to the café after carnival season they were visited by an aristocrat, Count Chikoff, who made them an offer they couldn't refuse: 6000 pesos a month to play at the Vogue Club, which ran tea dances for high society.

Success seemed assured, but Pedro Maffia and Luis Petrucelli were annoyed that the band was advertised under Julio's name and quit. Maffia was persuaded to rejoin at the last moment but only because he had lost a lot of money gambling. The second bandoneón was Pedro Láurenz. It was not an easy start for Láurenz: Maffia was famously taciturn. Julio writes[16]:

> *Maffia barely deigned to greet Láurenz, and "El negro" Thompson looked him up and down, while Francisco, who knew his worth, smiled, wondering what would happen when the lid came off this closely watched pot. At the first beats of Láurenz, Maffia, looking sideways, could not hide his admiration.*

De Caro's place in the highest strata of society was now cemented. When the aristocracy organised a reception for the Prince of Wales at the Palais de Glace in April 1925, De Caro's orchestra was the one invited to play.

After such a long introduction, let's now listen to their 1927 recording of "**Flores negras**", composed by Francisco De Caro. Immediately one hears the unusual tone of Julio De Caro's violin – more on this in a moment – whilst behind it the second violin plays a complex, shifting harmony. The melody is sent round all the instruments and the piano part, in the hands of Francisco, is particularly rich and complex, especially when you remember it's

[16] Roberto Selles, quoted on lptango.com.ar http://www.lptango.com.ar/index.php?option=com_content&id=253 (accessed 20th June 2012)

1927. A lot is made of Julio De Caro's genius but the band was very nearly named after Francisco. His contribution is immense.

De Caro's famous cornet violin

Photographs of Julio De Caro show him playing what looks like a violin with a horn attached. These were called Stroh violins after their inventor. Examine a photograph and you will see that the 'violin' to which the horn is attached is not a normal violin at all. The Stroh was created in the days before microphones with one intention: to make more volume. It consists of little more than a fingering board with a horn and tone box attached to a metal bridge. The tone is not sweet, and the amplification produced by the horn makes it sound quite nasal. They were also expensive.

The cornet violin was not De Caro's idea. This is a very strange story. Apparently the famous American jazz violinist Paul Whiteman heard one of De Caro's tangos playing at the Victor studios and was so impressed that he arranged for one of his cornet violins to be delivered to De Caro, thinking that its different tonality would suit De Caro's innovative sound. (Before the introduction of electric recording Stroh's were sometimes substituted for normal violins by jazz musicians because of the extra volume). In 1925, Mr Scheney, president of the Victor Company, presented it to De Caro on a visit to Buenos Aires. However as far as we can tell the violin was not a gift: Scheney deducted the cost of the instrument from De Caro's royalties.

By all accounts, De Caro was not keen on the instrument at first but he soon came to love it and used it exclusively thereafter. Today we identify the cornet violin with him.

De Caro across the decades

Julio De Caro was not really concerned with dancing but, in a few short years at the end of the 1920s, the work of the De Caro brothers changed the entire landscape of tango. Moving into the 1930s, the consensus is that he began to lose his way. Certainly it's hard to know what to make, for instance, of the wild dynamics of 1935's "**Taba calzada**".

The success of D'Arienzo, who turned his back on De Caro's innovations in his quest to make tango vigorous and danceable, seems to have disoriented De Caro completely. If the milonga "**Saca chispas**" (1938) is designed for dancers then it's tremendously successful, but with a work such as 1940's "**Catamarca**" it's hard to be sure which audience he is aiming for. That's not to discount this music, but it seems to be becoming more successful in the milongas and valses than in the tangos – not something one expects to say about Julio De Caro. Have a listen to the 1943 vals "**Sorpresa de novia**" and see if you agree.

De Caro retired after making this recording, at the height of the tango boom. It must have been an extraordinary event at the time. He returned in 1949, when tango was beginning its decline as the dominant popular art form of Buenos Aires, in order to show everyone how it was done. These final sides are truly magnificent: listen for instance to the final rendition of "**Flores negras**" from 1952. The music has more warmth: how can that be? Something else has happened in the meantime: Osvaldo Pugliese had shown De Caro another way of playing his own music.

Julio De Caro: what to listen to

De Caro's recordings fall into four periods:

1. 1924-1928: the sextet recordings on Victor. For these, get the 'Tango Collection' CD. Note that De Caro always referred to his group as an orchestra, even when it had only six members.
2. 1929-1932: sextet recordings on Brunswick (the least important period) – no CD available.
3. 1935-1943 (Victor): get 'Bien jaileife' on 'Reliquias' (*jaileife* is the *lunfardo* transliteration of the English "high life"!) and then if you want more, the mp3 album from DyM 'el candombe'.

4. 1949-1953 (Odeón): get 'Tangos de Rompe y Raje' on 'Reliquias'. This just tops the album in the 'From Argentina to the World' series for its inclusion of a few vocals with Orlando Verri. Their rendition of "**Mi dolor**" is simply outstanding.

Don't go overboard with a De Caro collection: look hard enough and it's possible to find a lot of material from the late 1920s and early 1930s, but you won't listen to most of it more than once.

CD	RGS	1641	Tango Collection – Julio De Caro	2011
CD	DBN	495376	Tangos de rompe y raje	1998
CD	DBN	541697	Bien jaileife	2002
mp3	DyM	160	Tango Classics 160 – el candombe	2010

21 / OTV and the house orchestras: Orquesta Típica Sony, anyone?

Listening guide

ORQUESTA ADOLFO CARABELLI

1/ Alma (1932)

ORQUESTA TÍPICA VICTOR

2/ C.T.V. (1932)

3/ Vieja calesita (1929) estribillo: Luís Díaz

ORQUESTA TÍPICA LOS PROVINCIANOS

4/ El distinguido ciudadano (1932)

TRÍO CIRIACO ORTIZ

5/ Soledad (v) (1933)

Today we would be rather surprised to hear that EMI or Sony had formed their own orchestra, but back in the early 20th century it was quite common for record companies to have their own house orchestras. The most successful and enduring of these was the **Orquesta Típica Victor**, launched by Victor in 1925 to try and compete with Max Glucksmann's Odeón label which had all the most successful stars of the day signed as exclusive artists: Francisco Canaro, Roberto Firpo and of course the great Carlos Gardel. It would later be joined by the **Orquesta Típica Columbia** and my own favourite, the sadly short lived **Orquesta Típica Brunswick**.

The Típica Victor, or **OTV** for short, recorded 459 numbers, nearly all before the end of 1941 by which time the idea of a house orchestra was obsolete. These house orchestras only made recordings; they never performed in public. The musicians were drawn from the ranks of those contracted to the label with a fixed director appointed by the record company. This was the bandoneonista Luis Petrucelli, but then in 1926 Petrucelli went to the USA to play bandoneón for Canaro. In his stead, Victor hired **Adolfo Carabelli**.

Now curiously, Carabelli formed his own orchestra at the same time which also only made recordings. This orchestra played jazz and tango, in that order.

These groups have the same members so it's not unreasonable to think they might have a similar sound. In particular, RCA Victor had a brilliant violinist in the person of Elvino Vardaro. His distinctive tone dominates the opening of the classic "**Alma**". As arrangements go, this sounds little different to what the OTV was doing provided we compare recordings from the same year (1932), for instance their "**C.T.V.**". Even the record companies get confused: on the now deleted 'RCA Victor 100 Años' Típica Victor CD, BMG printed the Carabelli "**Rodríguez Peña**" by mistake.

The OTV's tango recordings cover a much longer period of time than Carabelli's and are much more numerous, so it should come as no surprise to learn that the OTV has more variety. For a rather different style, try 1929's "**Vieja calesita**". This is much more focussed on the beat, and was one of the favourite tracks of the *milonguero* couple Rodolfo & Maria Cieri for their *canyengue* performances.

The Típica Victor ground to a halt in 1935, making only two recordings. Victor then give the baton to the bandoneonista Federico Scorticati, who remained in charge until the orchestra made what seemed to be its final recordings in 1941. By this time tango orchestras were everywhere and the need for a house orchestra had all but vanished. Nevertheless, the orchestra had a final flourish – 18 tracks recorded in 1943-1944, for which the group was directed by the pianist Mario Maurano.

Ciriaco Ortiz

Beginning in 1931 the bandoneón player **Ciriaco Ortiz**, a member of the orchestra since the beginning, made 34 recordings with the Victor house orchestra under the name **Orquesta Típica Los Provincianos**. Most of these date from the years 1931-1934. Now, Ciriaco Ortiz was never the director of the OTV. At this time Carabelli was still the director and the orchestra was recording prolifically under its own name. Here's the 64,000 Euro question: does it sound like the OTV? Well, yes it does, but comparing their recordings to the OTV's from the same years, something interesting emerges: the recordings of Los Provincianos are often more sophisticated musically. If you like: they are better. I like to think that Ciriaco Ortiz forces Carabelli to raise his game.

A case in point is the daring arrangement of "**El distinguido ciudadano**". This is recorded in 1932, the same year as the Carabelli track we listened to. Quite near the beginning Ortiz plays a long unaccompanied bandoneón variation, and when the orchestra returns, the violin – none other than Elvino Vardaro – steals the show, playing one passage just with the accompaniment of the double bass, the left hand of the piano and what sounds very much like a snare drum. Vardaro must have been thrilled to play such an arrangement which takes full advantage of the fact that the band aren't playing live before dancers. Even so, it nearly works as a dance piece – the unaccompanied bandoneón solo is just a bit too long to be comfortable for dancing.

Ortiz's bandoneón playing can be heard to even better effect in the trio he formed with the guitarists Andrés Menéndez and Vicente Spina (the composer of the classic vals "Tu olvido"). In these trio recordings one can hear a unique tone and phrasing. Ciriaco was not a *porteño* – he was born in a village in the province of Córdoba, and what you can hear in his playing is something of the feeling of the countryside. In particular, the mournful air of the vals  "**Soledad**" – Ciriaco's own composition – reminds me of the way that Atahualpa Yupanqui evokes the vastness and the silence of the Argentinean pampas. The trio recordings are intimate and tender and also very danceable.

The house orchestras on CD: what to listen to

Please don't ignore the Ciriaco Ortiz CD: it's spectacular. As for the Carabelli CD, only ten numbers are tangos and valses but it's the only CD in print.

Euro	17014	Colección 78 RPM: OTV 1930/1944	2005
Euro	17021	Colección 78 RPM 2: OTV 1929/1944	2005
Euro	17024	Colección 78 RPM 2: Los Provincianos / Trío Ciriaco Ortiz	2005
Euro	17043	Colección 78 RPM: "Mi evocación" Adolfo Carabelli 1927/1935	2005
DyM	3008	Que bonboncito	2002

The DyM CD was mentioned previously when we talked about the sextets; it has some tracks by the **Típica Brunswick**.

22/ Juan Maglio: the ultimate old-timer

Listening guide

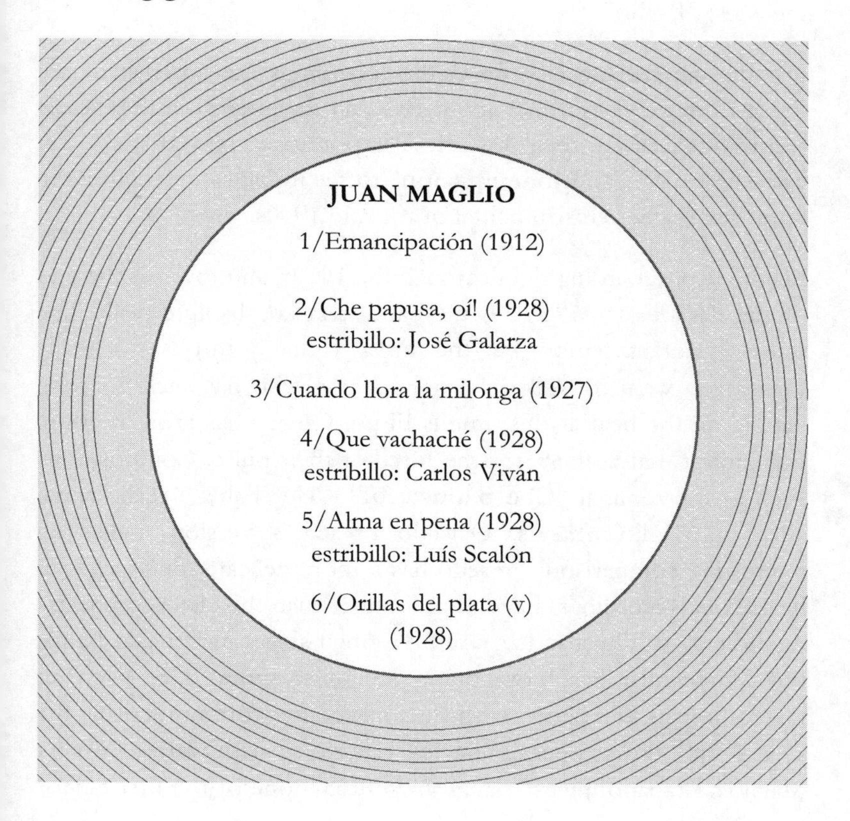

Please note: you will see other names for these vocalists on CDs and elsewhere. The identity of the vocalist was not normally printed on the label. These listings have been corrected by the work of a number of researchers over many years and are our best guess at the time of writing.

In the first decade of the 20th century there were three great bandoneón players: Eduardo Arolas, Genaro Esposito – both of whom went to Europe – and Vicente Greco. Greco's was the most famous orchestra until about 1912 when he was supplanted by Juan Maglio, nicknamed Pacho (a corruption of the Italian *pazzo*, crazy). In those days, Maglio was so successful and his recordings so popular that people walked into a record shop and simply asked for the latest "Pacho".

For the tango dancer of today the recordings that interest us are those from no earlier than about 1926, so the interest in these early recordings lies in their historical importance. Nevertheless, try listening to 1912's "**Emancipación**" to see if you can recognise the immortal Pugliese instrumental of the mid 1950s.

Maglio kept recording right through the 1920s, and towards the end of the decade (say 1928-29) the band is at an absolute peak. The music is not up-tempo, but the *compás* veritably throbs – it really makes you want to walk. The only person who has such a strong handle on the beat at this time is Firpo. Canaro has more rhythm, but cannot match them for the force of their pulse. Compositions such as the seminal "**Che papusa, oi**" ("Hey babe!") really come alive in Maglio's hands. Osvaldo Fresedo's version makes an interesting comparison. Fresedo has a more delicate touch, even if his sextet recordings have more pulse than his later orchestra recordings, and he also has a more refined singer in Ernesto Famá, but Maglio just has more pulse. He must surely have been an inspiration to D'Arienzo with his unswerving commitment to the 2 x 4 and the peppering of his repertoire with valses. Wasn't Maglio's "Sábado inglés" (English Saturday) one of the first tangos that D'Arienzo recorded?

Some of these arrangements are really quite sophisticated for an orchestra that is often dismissed on the grounds that it was out-of-date. Let's listen for instance to 1927's "**Cuando llora la milonga**". After a brief introduction, the slow melody opens on the bandoneóns but listen closely and there's a lot going on underneath:

pizzicato in the violins, and some playful work in the right-hand of the piano. They must have been fantastic live.

Of Maglio's vocalists **Carlos Viván** was by far the best but the important thing about this orchestra is not quality of the singing, it's their great pulse. Maglio runs a tight ship in order to deliver that and rarely lets himself rip as a soloist; see if you can find "En un rincón de café" for an astonishing bandoneón solo that makes clear why he was considered one of the best bandoneón players in Buenos Aires in the early days. We've also including one of his valses, "**Orillas del Plata**" ("On the banks of the River Plate"), another of his own compositions with a surprisingly syncopated melody.

Maglio's recordings peter out in the early thirties. He didn't retire, although his music wasn't really developing and his recording sessions were becoming less frequent. One of the real old timers, Maglio passed away in 1934 aged just 53. It's impossible to know how he would have fared under the D'Arienzo revolution of 1935 and during the subsequent Golden Decade of the 1940s, but the weight of the evidence is that he would have been left behind.

Despite these speculations, Juan Maglio left behind a huge legacy both as a composer and as a performer. His recordings were prolific: Lefcovich's discography has 754, but some say he cut almost 900 tracks.

Juan Maglio – what to listen to

For most people the early recordings from 1912 will be for interest only – try to listen to his sides from 1927 onwards. There is very little available on commercial CD.

el bandoneón	EBCD-86	Sábado inglés	1996
Euro	EU-17052	Colección 78 RPM: "La guardia vieja" 1927-1932	2010

The other orchestras: a summary

Canaro: a giant of the 1930s who ran out of inspiration when the shift to the orchestra singer arrived in 1938. Wonderful when he balanced his strong beat with softer vocalists (Charlo, Maida). Key musician: Minotto (bandoneón).

Caló: great musicianship, simple phrases. Elegance and romance, above all with the smooth voice of Raul Berón. Pianist: Osmar Maderna

D'Agostino/Vargas: a great partnership. Understated. Kept a sparse texture but gave lots of attention to the rhythm, making it a favourite of dancers. Careful and unique choice of repertoire, nostalgic. Pianist: D'Agostino himself.

Biagi: extreme and unpredictable *marcato*, emphasising the off-beat.

Tanturi: a rhythmic orchestra, although less extremely so than D'Arienzo, which was able to incorporate melody and lyricism into its approach. Had two great singers, **Alberto Castillo** and **Enrique Campos**. Pianist: Tanturi himself.

Láurenz: a musical genius, years ahead of his time. Famous for his virtuoso bandoneón playing. Inaugurated the Golden Decade with his classic "**Arrabal**".

Donato: irrepressible, cheeky fun, with an accordion in the bandoneón section and lots of playful pizzicato in the violins. Playful and upbeat even in his earliest recordings.

Maglio: a pioneer who made wonderful music for dancing with a rock-steady beat in the years 1926-34, even if he was by then well past his peak.

Firpo: alongside Canaro, an early innovator and a giant of the old guard. A wonderful orchestra which combined softness with strength but failed to adapt to the new wave.

Lomuto: a more muscular, meatier version of Canaro. Solid and conservative.

De Caro: greatly increased the sophistication of tango music. Not really a dance band, but paved the way for Pugliese.

Fresedo: posh tango, wonderful with Ray but often too sugary and airy in his later recordings. The earlier sextet recordings are surprising full bodied.

OTV: only met for studio recordings. Excellent musicianship and arrangements, largely in the old style.

De Angelis: A light romantic orchestra, remembered for the vocal partnership of Carlos Dante and Julio Martel rather than for its musicianship.

Demare: a lush romantic sound, relatively few recordings.

Part 4

The "big four" orchestras in depth

23 / Juan D'Arienzo: after the big bang

Listening guide

ORQUESTA
JUAN D'ARIENZO

1/ Uno (1943) canta: Héctor Mauré
2/ Amarras (1944) canta: Héctor Mauré
3/ El romántico (1944)

4/ Cartón junao (1947) canta: Alberto Echagüe

5/ Canaro en París (1950)
6/ Tucumán (1951) 7/ La cumparsita (1951)
8/ El simpático (1951) 9/ Yapeyú (1951)
10/ El puntazo (1952) 11/ Loca (1955)
12/ Más grande que nunca (1958)
13/ Gran Hotel Victoria (1966)
14/ 9 de Julio (1966)

In our earlier introduction to Juan D'Arienzo we looked at his explosion onto the musical scene at the end of 1935. Instrumental in that was the serendipitous incorporation of pianist Rodolfo Biagi.

Although Biagi's departure in 1938 knocked D'Arienzo back, new man Juan Polito was eventually able to do a fair job of copying the Biagi style. The band was riding the crest of a wave of popularity when, in March 1940, D'Arienzo lost his entire orchestra, including singer Alberto Echagüe, as Polito split to form his own outfit.

Naturally this was a set-back but D'Arienzo persuaded bandoneonista Héctor Varela to put his new orchestra at D'Arienzo's disposal, recruited Cayetano Puglisi as violinist, and placed an 18-year-old Fulvio Salamanca in the pianist's chair. The new orchestra was even more successful than the old one, but listening to it we can hear that something is missing: the presence of Alberto Echagüe. D'Arienzo recruited two singers to fill the void left by Echagüe's departure: Alberto Reynal and Carlos Casares. Neither of them has the quality or the charisma of their predecessor and for many months the band records a lower proportion of vocal numbers. By the end of the year Casares is gone. His replacement at the end of 1940 was rising young star **Héctor Mauré**.

Now I really wonder if D'Arienzo knew what he was doing when he invited Mauré into his orchestra, because Mauré's presence was going to have a huge impact on the direction in which the orchestra developed. It's the end of 1940. It's a year since Di Sarli formed his new orchestra and Troilo has arrived on the scene with the wonderful Francisco Fiorentino on vocals. Both the vocalist and the lyric are becoming more and more important and Héctor Mauré is the right man for the job.

There's only one problem: the D'Arienzo orchestra is founded on rhythm and not on lyricism. Mauré is sophisticated, yet the D'Arienzo style identifies with the street. It's a fascinating collision of styles. Between December 1940 and July 1944 Mauré will record 50 numbers with D'Arienzo and you can hear the development unfold on their discs. Mauré responds to the influence of the times, taking more and more space and seemingly forcing the orchestra into ever more nuanced interpretations. Some of those performances are masterpieces: their version of Discépolo's "**Uno**" is perhaps the greatest ever recorded.  The music swells and tumbles in great tides in a most un-D'Arienzo like manner. Their final number together, "**Amarras**", is completely of its time and yet  challenges our notion of D'Arienzo even further. The music is sensitive, almost introverted but listen underneath and it is clearly still D'Arienzo.

Brilliant as this work is, you can see what's coming. This is not the D'Arienzo blueprint, and Mauré has to go. The writing is on the wall in the summer of 1944 when D'Arienzo tempts Echagüe back. These two singers just don't go together, and by the end of the year Mauré is gone, replaced by Armando Laborde. Some tango historians talk about a new golden age for the orchestra, but for the dancer – despite some outstanding recordings such as the instrumental "**El romántico**" and the impossible to find "**Color cielo**" –  our interest in the orchestra's output diminishes with this change. You'll find very few CDs covering the period from the departure of Mauré until the end of the decade. I'm not so fond of this period, so instead of following my recommendations, let's take the advice of a top Japanese collector who rates "**Carton junao**" as one of his  top five D'Arienzo tracks ever. I do find the music has emotion but it doesn't make me want to dance.

1950: the sleeping dragon wakes

At the beginning of 1950 something very special happens to the D'Arienzo orchestra. It seems that they return from a long summer break with renewed vigour. On their first session back in the studio they record seven numbers, just like the good old days, including stunning new versions of "**El internado**" and "**Canaro en París**".   Five more tracks follow just ten days later. At this point Varela – first bandoneón and arranger – quits to form his own orchestra after ten years with D'Arienzo. Now D'Arienzo has suffered such setbacks before and knows how to survive them. He appoints Salamanca (his pianist) as arranger and the orchestra is out of the studio for some months as it re-groups. When they return they are even stronger than before, unleashing a string of top-notch instru-mental hits: "**Tucumán**", "**Don Juan**", "**El simpático**", "**Yapeyú**" and most especially the seminal 1951 recording of "**La cumparsita**" (in a new arrangement) which for my money is the best of their seven recordings of this standard.

In 1952 the band can't quite keep up this level of creativity but they still release the devastating "**El puntazo**". When tape masters arrive at the end of 1954, D'Arienzo re-records all of his current hits: listen to the new recording of "El internado" to hear just how good it sounds. From here on to the end of the decade it is mostly entirely forgettable vocals, but don't let that blind you to the occasional work of genius such as the 1955 recording of "**Loca**" ("Crazy") or 1958's "**Mas grande que nunca**" ("Better than ever"). I think these are some of D'Arienzo's most exciting tangos and can't understand why they aren't regularly chosen by show dancers. Maybe they just haven't heard them.

In 1957 Echagüe and Laborde left the orchestra and D'Arienzo hired two new singers, Jorge Valdéz and Mario Bustos. Their style veers towards the camp and the instrumentals become fewer and fewer. Our interest in the orchestra appears to be on the wane when a new technical innovation has huge consequences for tango music. That innovation: stereo.

The stereo era: Tango for Export

At a time when interest in tango had shrunk in Argentina, the executives at RCA where hopeful that the new stereo technology could create a new market for tango music abroad. Accordingly they decided to record some albums of instrumental tangos purely for the export market. These albums were called 'Tango for Export', and this was also the term used twenty years later to describe the stage tango that reignited interest in tango abroad in shows such as 'Tango Argentino', giving birth to the tango revival.

D'Arienzo's arrangements of "La cumparsita"

D'Arienzo recorded "La cumparsita" seven times but it wasn't until 1951 that the piece found its final shape.

The 1928 version begins with five sections, the last being the one string violin solo that we so associate with D'Arienzo. The 1935 version adds the new bandoneón *variación* of Luis Moresco. For the 1943 version D'Arienzo swaps the positions of the bandoneón *variación* and the previous violin *variación*, but it doesn't quite work: when the violin *variación* appears the energy of the piece drops. This is solved by the insertion in 1951 of a stunning new bandoneón *variación*, taking the piece out to almost four minutes in length. Here are the different versions mapped out - (A = verse music, B = chorus music):

<table>
<tr><td>1928</td><td>A</td><td>B</td><td>A′
Vocal</td><td>B′
Piano</td><td></td><td></td><td></td><td>A′
Violin</td></tr>
<tr><td>1935</td><td>A</td><td>B</td><td>A′
Violin</td><td>B′
Piano</td><td></td><td>A′
Bando</td><td>A′
Piano</td><td>A
Violin</td></tr>
<tr><td>1943</td><td>A</td><td>B</td><td>A′
Bando</td><td>B′
Piano</td><td></td><td>A′
Violin</td><td>A′
Piano</td><td>A
Violin</td></tr>
<tr><td>1951
1963</td><td>A</td><td>B</td><td>A′
Bando</td><td>B′
Piano</td><td>A″
Bando</td><td>A′
Violin</td><td>A′
Piano</td><td>A
Violin</td></tr>
<tr><td>1971</td><td>A</td><td>B</td><td>A′
Bando</td><td>B′
Piano</td><td>A″
Bando</td><td>A‴
Violin</td><td>A′
Piano</td><td>A
Violin</td></tr>
</table>

The 1963 version from the 'Tango for Export' years is the same arrangement but taken more slowly, such that it lasts four minutes. Compared to the 1951 version it lacks energy – not something one often says about the king of the beat.

In 1971 D'Arienzo made a new arrangement of "La cumparsita". As a performance the 1951 recording has the edge but as an arrangement the new version may be his best. After the "new" bandoneón *variación*, D'Arienzo takes us completely by surprise: the violin part is substituted for a new one in which the violins play not low on the fourth (base) string, but very high on the first string. The notes fly upwards and disappear into silence, leaving us suspended in mid-air until the piano comes to rescue us. Genius.

I'm not sure how successful these albums were at the time in achieving their aim of opening new markets for tango music. For us, their significance is that they re-focussed tango on the instrumental numbers. The Tango for Export albums of both D'Arienzo and Troilo are still in print and whilst the Troilo numbers come across more as concert music, the D'Arienzo numbers are hugely enjoyable – perhaps even more now than in their day.

D'Arienzo's first 'Tango for Export' album is pretty good but volume 2 (1966) is simply outstanding. D'Arienzo is still experimenting and finding new ideas. In "**Gran Hotel Victoria**" the music completely disappears in the middle of the track, leaving you to count the beats until it comes back – try it! (You might like to compare it to the 1935 "**Hotel Victoria**" just to see how far the band has come). From the same album I also really enjoy the new version of "**9 de julio**" which permits itself a subtlety that we haven't heard before.

D'Arienzo's recording career lasted until 1975 and he continued to be a creative force until the end: the wonderful "**Este es el rey**", for example, dates from 1971. He passed away in January 1976.

In an interview given a month before his death he had this to say[17]

> *"If musicians turned back to the purity of 2 x 4, the passion for our music would come again and, thanks to the modern media of broadcasting, we would reach world importance".*

This interview is normally quoted pejoratively as an example of D'Arienzo's intransigence in the face of the "evolution" of tango. I couldn't agree more about D'Arienzo's stubbornness, except that as a dancer I feel that this is a sign of his commitment to his musical vision – a vision that sustained him throughout his lifetime and continues to nourish us today, long after his death.

---

[17] "Tango y Lunfardo" Nº 132, op. cit

D'Arienzo after the big bang: what to listen to

For the 40s sides there are now quite a few CDs and you'll need all of these just for the Héctor Mauré tracks. There are four CDs on Euro Records, whilst the next two volumes of Sony-BMG's 'Homenaje en Sony BMG' present more interesting material.

For the 1950s it's the instrumentals we want, not the vocals. The best place to start by far is the cracking Solo Tango album 'Instrumental vol.1' – a re-print of the 'FM Tango' album first published in 1992. (There were four albums in that series, hence the name). You can find more on the neglected 'Dos maestros, dos estilos' on Euro Records, which also has some rare instrumentals of Carlos Di Sarli. Euro know we don't really want the vocals: the spine confesses, *Selección bailable*, danceable selection. After this we have to get the next two CDs of 'Homenaje en Sony BMG'. These have far too many vocal tracks, but what can you do?

For the later 'Tango for export' era, begin with the BMG album 'El rey del compás'. This has the 1971 "**La cumparsita**" and the best transfer of "**Este es el rey**". This CD has been continuously in-print since 1993, making it perhaps the longest lived tango CD. There are at least three CDs with this title, so be careful. This is the one with a night-time photograph of a street in Buenos Aires on the cover – printed back-to-front!

BMG	71372	Solo Tango Instrumental vol.1	2000
BMG	669334	El rey del compás (1941-1943)	2005
BMG	669339	Corrientes y Esmeralda (1944-1949)	2005
Euro	17009	Juan D'Arienzo 1940/1942	2005
Euro	17010	Juan D'Arienzo 1941/1944	2005
Euro	17011	Juan D'Arienzo 1944/1949	2005
Euro	17040	Juan D'Arienzo 1947/1952	2005
Euro	17019	Archivo RCA – Dos maestros, dos estilos (Selección bailable)	2003
BMG	ECD 1100	El rey del compás	1993
BMG	669340	Bien Pulenta (1950-1952)	2005
BMG	669344	Mucho Mucho (1953-1954)	2005

24/ Carlos Di Sarli
The rise of melody

Listening guide

ORQUESTA
CARLOS DI SARLI

1/ Milonguero viejo (1940)
2/ Milonguero viejo (1944)
3/ Milonguero viejo (1951)
4/ Milonguero viejo (1955)

5/ Indio manso (1958)

6/ Verdemar (1943) canta: Roberto Rufino
7/ La capilla blanca (1944) canta: Alberto Podestá
8/ Porteño y bailarín (1945) canta: Jorge Durán
9/ Duelo criollo (1953) canta: Mario Pomar
10/ La novia del mar (1953) canta: Oscar Serpa
11/ Tormenta (1954) canta: Mario Pomar
12/ Derrotado (1956) canta:
Roberto Florio

By now you may have noticed a pattern emerging in the career of an orchestra, a pattern that reflects the wider social changes taking place in Argentina in the 1940s. In most cases, once the bandleader has succeeded in finding his "sound", the early recordings are the best ones. As time runs on the music becomes more sophisticated but less danceable. Alongside the increasing importance of the lyric, the singer becomes de-integrated from the orchestra, further reducing the effectiveness of the whole as dance music.

In the case of Carlos Di Sarli much of this doesn't happen. His music continues to develop, and he's not immune to the developments taking place around him, but neither diminish the effectiveness of his work as dance music. His 50s recordings are played almost as much as his 40s ones, and some feel that his early 50s recordings on the TK label are his best.

Whenever I think about the development of Di Sarli's music over the decades I am always reminded of Debussy's piano piece, "La Cathedrale Engloutie" ("The Submerged Cathedral"). There is a legend in the North of France that there once existed a city on the Breton coast called Ys that was swallowed by the ocean. In one version of this legend, it was told that at sunrise the Cathedral would rise from the sea and toll its bells before sinking back into the waters. All of this is depicted in Debussy's piece.

"The Submerged Cathedral" speaks to me as a metaphor for the unfolding of Di Sarli's music which, over the decades, displays an ever-increasing emphasis not on the lyric but on the melody, slowly submerging the rhythm of the music in a great melodic wash. This is not a sudden change but a constant and gradual development over his entire musical career, evincing an inner musical conception to which he remained faithful. The genius of Di Sarli is that, just like the sunken Cathedral, the underlying structure is never lost.

Di Sarli retired on a number of occasions, making it easy to divide his recording career into distinct periods. It's possible to follow his style through these periods because he recorded a number of pieces several times.

1. 1939-1948: RCA Victor. 158 numbers
2. 1951-1954: TK. 84 numbers
3. 1954-1958: RCA Victor. 80 numbers
4. 1958: Polygram. 14 numbers (1 LP).

The final album on Polygram represents the culmination of his life's work, and no serious collection of tango music is complete without it, but style wise it's not so different from the period on RCA Victor which precedes it. Di Sarli's first stint with RCA Victor however is a long one. We've already seen and heard how much the music changed in that time. Is there a Di Sarli track we can find recorded twice in this period, say once near the beginning and once near the end, as well as in the TK and later RCA Victor sessions?

There is, just one, and appropriately enough it's Di Sarli's own composition, "**Milonguero viejo**" which he recorded in 1940, 1944, 1951 and 1955. (The "old milonguero" of the title is a tribute to Osvaldo Fresedo, who gave him his start in Buenos Aires).

Listen through all four versions and the first thing that strikes you is how alike they sound. The arrangements are very similar, and Di Sarli uses the instruments in the same way each time, the way he always uses them: violins dominating, being used for both staccato and legato, with Di Sarli's piano providing delicate fills between the phrases and strong bass during them.

On the other hand, listen to each version all the way through and one finds that the effect that the music has is quite different. The pace slows dramatically: 73 bpm (beats per minute) in the first recording, then 63, 60 and finally 59bpm. The first version stands out as more urgent than the others, but it's not just that: the melody is intensifying. How is it possible that the melody gets so much stronger?

A big part of the answer is that the number of violins is going up. In his 1939 orchestra Di Sarli had only three violins, soon expanding to the usual four, with the number of bandoneóns being the same. The 1951 orchestra on the other hand had six violins and five bandoneóns. The 1954 orchestra is the same orchestra, only the record label having changed.

In 1956 virtually Di Sarli's entire band (including his loyal first violin Roberto Guisado) left him so they could work in the carnival dances, which were much better paid, and he then formed a new orchestra of five violins and four bandoneóns. In 1957 Guisado and one other violin returned, and one of the bandoneóns, so the orchestra was now seven violins and five bandoneóns. The violin section was expanded to eight in 1958, an unforgettable experience for those who attended the carnival dances of 1959.

Year	Violins	Bandoneóns
1939	3	3
1940? - 1948	4	4
1951 - 1955	6	5
1956	5	4
1957 - 1958	7	5
1958 - 1959	8	5

Carlos Di Sarli: more violins, please

What you can see here is that not only is the number of violins increasing, giving the Di Sarli melody engine more power, but that the balance with the bandoneóns is changing. Di Sarli's bandoneóns don't sound as though they are doing anything, but they are: they are adding the rhythmic drive for the dancers.

The same goes for the double bass and the piano. The left hand of the piano and the double bass provide the bass notes of a tango orchestra and give it its walking drive. There is still only one double bass and of course only one piano, so relatively they have less punch. Di Sarli has gone from a 3-3-1-1 formation (3 violins, 3 bandoneóns, 1 double bass, 1 piano) to 8-5-1-1. This delivers incredible melodic lines but has less overt rhythmic strength.

The rest of the answer lies in the seemingly inevitable slowing of the music that takes place through the years. In Di Sarli's case the optimum pace for the dancer is probably the one in the early 1950s, whilst he is on the TK label. This is a pity, because the sound on the TK recordings is not very good.

Di Sarli's singers

Di Sarli was well served by a series of excellent and well-chosen vocalists. We've already met **Roberto Rufino** who sang with the orchestra for a little over three years. When we think of Rufino it's almost impossible not to think of "**Corazón**" but we mustn't forget the slower paced tracks he recorded towards the end of his tenure such as the immortal "**Verdemar**".

Di Sarli's second singer was of course **Alberto Podestá**. He has less pyrotechnics than Rufino and the development is rather like Tanturi's evolution when Alberto Castillo was replaced by Enrique Campos: not as explosive, but possibly even better for dancing. Podestá is Di Sarli's most subtle singer. From a string of hits we've selected 1944's "**La capilla blanca**" to demonstrate the supreme good taste of this combination. When the chorus comes, Podestá still gets to hold the high note the way he did with Láurenz on "**Alma del bohemia**".

The next singer to enter the ranks of the orchestra was **Jorge Durán**. With his dark baritone, Durán was more of a departure for Di Sarli who showed himself well ahead of the curve here: it would be years before the other big orchestras experimented with these voices. We've selected their first recording together, "**Que no sepan las estrellas**". The rhythmic opening gives way to beautiful melodies, first in the orchestra and then of course in Durán's regal voice. These recordings deserve to be much better known.

In the early 50s Di Sarli was working with two new singers, **Mario Pomar** and **Oscar Serpa**. Pomar has already sung with the OTV but you wouldn't know it because at that time he hadn't adopted his stage name. He appears in their discography as Mario Corrales.

Both Pomar and Serpa had a series of huge hits with Di Sarli. Pomar's rendition of "**Duelo criollo**" is a great example of the sound the orchestra developed in the early 50s: much slower in pace than the 40s style, but still with a strong walking beat. The interplay between the violins and the voice is outstanding.

Serpa's voice is more unusual with a tone that is truly unique amongst tango vocalists. His smooth and expressive phrasing is said to be typical of the singers from his native district, Cuyo (in the province of Mendoza). These qualities are easy to appreciate in his 1953 version of "**La novia del mar**".

The TK label used low quality materials resulting in a frustratingly inferior standard in its recorded sound: poorer even than the standards of the 1940s. In 1954 Di Sarli decided he'd had enough of these limitations and switched back to RCA Victor which was now using tape masters. The improvement in the sound fidelity was dramatic: these tangos sound as if they were recorded yesterday.

Everyone knows the instrumentals but the vocal numbers are also very fine. The first one I heard was Pomar's 1954 recording of the Discépolo classic "**Tormenta**". This sends shivers up my spine and I just can't take the much better known version by Canaro seriously any more. The ways the violins build underneath Pomar's voice is just sensational.

When Di Sarli lost his orchestra at the end of 1955 (they wanted to play at the carnival dances, remember?) he lost his singers too. Of the replacements, the stand-out is the passionate Roberto Florio. Listen for instance to 1956's "**Derrotado**" ("Defeated"), once again with incredible swelling phrases in the violins, and tell me you are not moved.

Que mufa ché! Tango & superstition

The Argentines are a superstitious lot. There is a lunfardo word, *mufa*, which means 'bad luck' in the sense of being of ill omen.

Di Sarli's misfortunes began in 1944. In January of that year a huge earthquake had devastated the city of San Juan in the west of Argentina. Di Sarli refused to play for free at a benefit concert. The promoters were disgruntled and put it about that Di Sarli was *mufa*, bad luck. This slander was enthusiastically taken up by some of those who felt Di Sarli to be their competitor. As a result of this Di Sarli never got work in films, and consequently there is no footage of his orchestra performing. It's our loss.

In Argentina it was common for the bands to have an announcer who also doubled as a *glosador*, someone who read the *glosa* (poetic texts designed to be spoken rather than sung). In 1945 Di Sarli took on a certain well known announcer in this role. The two fell out and the presenter was sacked, but he took his revenge by amplifying the rumour that Di Sarli was *mufa*, to which he added the nickname "El tuerto", One-eye. Things got so bad that some people would cross the street to avoid him. Di Sarli, an upright man, never showed that he was bothered but the persistent slander took its toll. In 1948 Carlos Di Sarli simply gave up. He dissolved his orchestra and left the city for two years.

Despite the substantial damage caused to Di Sarli by these slanders he still managed to become one of the greatest orchestra leaders in the history of tango. Without them, his fame and his success would have been all the greater.

In November 1958 Di Sarli returned to the studio for the final time to record an LP for the Polygram label. The album opens with a new recording of "**Bahía Blanca**", one of five instrumentals on the disc. The famous version we usually hear is not this one but the one made with RCA Victor less than a year previously, and comparing the two recordings is revealing.

The new version is not as satisfying and a lot of this sounds to be the way that Polygram have recorded it. The recording is too forward and Di Sarli's piano seems heavier – is it too closely miked? I only mention all this to put into context the genius of the remaining instrumentals, particularly "**Indio manso**" and "**Una fija**".  These are simply outstanding, timeless classics. It's mind-boggling to think that they might have sounded a lot better if they had been recorded by RCA Victor.

These final tracks represent the distillation of a lifetime's work. Di Sarli is speaking to the dancers the whole time. He is the master not only of the melody but of the phrase. The music emerges from stillness and returns to it in repeated waves. These silences are not void, but full of potential. In these moments of suspension, our hearts are drawn to Di Sarli's crystalline piano work but don't forget to listen to the double bass, whose clear paired notes ("boom – boom…") announce the next movement, telling the dancers when to place their feet.

In the barrio of Villa Urquiza there was one *milonguero* who had a very strong reputation as a Di Sarli specialist, **Gerardo Portalea**. In Argentina many thought him the greatest interpreter of Di Sarli's music, if we can say such a thing. Towards the end of his life his health deteriorated and his demonstrations became fewer and fewer, but there is one video shot at the club Sin Rumbo. The piece he chose to dance to for this final performance? "**Indio manso**".

Di Sarli's final performances were at the carnival dances of 1959. Night after night, thousands of people pressed against the stage, too overwhelmed by the force and power of a line of eight violins to be able to dance. No-one realised at the time, but these dances were to be a farewell: Carlos Di Sarli died of cancer the following January, a few days after his 57th birthday.

Carlos Di Sarli: what to listen to

In short: everything, although it's hard to find good fidelity versions of the early 50s numbers on TK, and Polygram can't be bothered to keep their album in print.

BMG	87490	RCA Victor 100 Años – Carlos Di Sarli	2001
TARG	41298	Sus primeros éxitos vol.1 (Rufino)	1996
TARG	41299	Sus primeros éxitos vol.2 (Podestá)	1996
TARG	63345	Instrumental vol.2	1998
TARG	63346	Sus primeros éxitos vol.3 (Rufino / Podestá)	1996
TARG	63347	Porteño y Bailarín (Durán)	1998
Euro	16010	Carlos Di Sarli y sus Cantores 1954/1958	2004
Euro	16023	Carlos Di Sarli con Jorge Durán y Roberto Florio (1956-1958)	2005
Euro	16028	Carlos Di Sarli (1954-1956)	2005
Euro	14031	"Tangueando Te Quiero" 1951-1953	2010

If we recommend 'Instrumental vol.2' on 'Tango Argentino', why not volume 1? Well, many of the tracks are ruined by a lot of reverberation, and the few good tracks can now be found on the Euro CD we recommended in the earlier Di Sarli chapter.

Carlos Di Sarli discography: the late instrumentals

A generation of tango dancers learned to dance to this music, which has a slow walking pace and a very clean sound. Out of 79 numbers recorded with RCA Victor in the years 1954-1957 just 23 were instrumental. Di Sari recorded an album on Polygram in 1958 with five more instrumentals, making 28 in total. Any tango collection worthy of the name should have them all, although the Polygram album is now hard to find.

the late instrumentals on RCA Victor

1	30.06.54	El choclo
2	30.06.54	A la gran muñeca
3	31.08.54	El amanecer
4	31.08.54	Organito de la tarde
5	08.09.54	Don José Maria
6	14.09.54	Cuidado con los 50
7	14.09.54	Tinta verde
8	28.09.54	La morocha
9	16.11.54	Bar Exposición
10	16.11.54	El once
11	31.01.55	Don Juan
12	31.01.55	El ingeniero
13	20.06.55	La cumparsita
14	20.06.55	Milonguero viejo
15	15.07.55	Comme il faut
16	15.07.55	Germaine
17	28.07.55	Los 33 orientales
18	23.02.56	Rodríguez Peña
19	23.02.56	El jagüel
20	07.03.56	Nueve puntos
21	19.12.56	Viviani
22	12.07.57	Cara sucia
23	21.11.57	Bahía Blanca

the late instrumentals – on Polygram

24	01.11.58	Una fija
25	01.11.58	El abrojo
26	01.11.58	Champagne tango
27	01.11.58	Indio manso
28	01.11.58	Bahía Blanca

25/ Osvaldo Pugliese: perhaps more than you think

Listening guide

ORQUESTA
OSVALDO PUGLIESE

1/ Emancipación (1955)

2/ La abandoné y no sabía (1944)
canta: Roberto Chanel

3/ Sin palabras (1947) canta: Alberto Morán
4/ Ventanita de arrabal (1949) canta: Jorge Vidal
5/ Pasional (1951) canta: Alberto Morán

6/ Tierra querida (1944) 7/ Flor de tango (1944)
8/ Derecho viejo (1945)

9/ De floreo (1950)
10/ A los amigos (1960)
11/ A Evaristo Carriego (1969)

Most people's introduction to Osvaldo Pugliese's music is not through his 1940s output that we spoke about earlier, but via a narrow selection of magnificent instrumentals from the late 1950s: for instance, "**Emancipación**", "**Nochero Soy**" and "**Gallo Ciego**". These are among the most intense tangos ever recorded. It's tempting to over-play them, and that's what happens in a lot of tango communities. Many of us have heard them so often that it's impossible to feel them afresh. Moreover, it creates a one-dimensional view of Pugliese and ends up putting a lot of people off his music. It's like drinking too much red wine and developing an allergy.

Pugliese's music is much broader than these fine but over-played instrumentals might suggest.

Pugliese's singers

For instance, it's often said that Pugliese didn't have good singers. What?

Pugliese's first recording was made in July 1943 with the voice of **Roberto Chanel** who had only recently joined the orchestra. It was a stroke of luck for Chanel: Pugliese's singers had just quit to join other orchestras which seemed to have better prospects. Pugliese-Chanel became one of the greatest combinations in the history of tango music, a pairing one can speak about in the same breath as Troilo-Fiorentino.

Chanel manages to combine the nasal tone and diction of a man of the street with a refinement that we don't associate with this style of singing. Alberto Echagüe (D'Arienzo's most successful singer) also has a street voice but Chanel's voice is much smoother. He has way more class. Pugliese-Chanel is just so good, and easier for the less experienced dancer than a lot of instrumental Pugliese because the structure is less challenging: in many instrumental pieces, Pugliese removes the *compás* altogether. I find it curious that Pugliese-Chanel isn't played more often.

Like all the great singers Chanel is already perfectly at home with the orchestra in his first recording, "**Farol**", which remains one of their classics. If you can manage it, do what I've just done and listen to all 31 of their recordings together. There are 29 solo recordings and two *a dúo* with Alberto Morán, who came on board in 1945.  Some of them really make my hair stand on end: try "**La abandoné y no sabía**" for an accessible introduction to this neglected material.

Alberto Morán came on board as Pugliese's second singer in 1945. Pugliese chose him as a contrast to Chanel and he couldn't have been more different: intense, dramatic and sensual. In "**Sin palabras**" (1947) we hear him at his peak. Morán sings every song as though it was his last and in later years his high-octane style damaged his voice. Wonderful as this tango is, we don't really feel like dancing and Morán's work is seldom heard at the milonga. Pugliese would later decide to exploit these qualities, but first we have to tell you about another of Pugliese's singers, **Jorge Vidal**. Let me just say, a fantastic voice, one of the best: a dark-toned baritone of tremendous power. He was not really Chanel's replacement, because when Chanel left to join Sassone in 1948 he was not replaced for nearly two years.

Towards the end of 1949, Osvaldo Ruggiero and Jorge Caldara (two of the bandoneóns in the Pugliese line-up) discovered **Jorge Vidal** singing at a café. Vidal was poor and penniless at this time, and would sleep on the floor of the café at night. One morning it was Don Osvaldo who shook him awake and offered him a job singing in his orchestra. Vidal accepted but stayed only a year, recording just eight immortal sides before going solo once again. I guess he was just too much of a free spirit. Vidal's sides with Pugliese are powerful and dramatic but still danceable. Particularly surprising is the repertoire. You'd never guess from the strong, modern delivery, but it turns out to be largely drawn from the  *guardia vieja*: "**Ventanita del arrabal**" was recorded by both Juan Maglio and Canaro in 1927. Gardel recorded it too, in 1930, along with another two of Vidal's hits, "**Barra querida**" and "**La**

cieguita". It's a mark of Jorge Vidal's greatness that his reputation now rests on material that was not typical for the orchestra and may even have seemed obsolete at the time.

After Vidal departed Pugliese embarked with Morán on what was called the "renewal of the tango song" but was really the beginning of the era of the soloist. Morán's voice was allowed to come to the fore. He was a star in his own right, backed by the Pugliese orchestra. With his dramatic, sensual voice he was a huge hit with the ladies: a friend recalls that the men would find themselves without partners whenever Morán sang because the ladies rushed to the stage. The tango which really defines this change is the iconic "**Pasional**" (1951). This is a work of such raging intensity that it bursts the borders of tango as we know it. It's wonderful, and at the same time it was the beginning of the end for tango dance music.

A rough guide to Pugliese's instrumentals

Pugliese once said, with characteristic modesty, that all he had wished to do when his orchestra appeared on the scene was to rescue the musical inheritance of Julio De Caro, which was in danger of being lost. Of course, we all know that he did much more than this. One way to track this is to listen to his recordings of compositions by Julio De Caro and the other members of his school.

1944's "**Tierra querida**" is a good place to start, and the track with which EMI opened their 1996 album 'De Caro Por Pugliese'. The recording is pure Pugliese. Listen to it side by side with De Caro's recording from 1927 and you'll hear that the arrangements are almost identical. How, then, is the feeling completely different? The Pugliese version breathes, it's full of life! In comparison, De Caro's music is dry and intellectual, designed to move the mind rather than the feet. You can hear the ideas in De Caro's music, and they are beautiful, but something is lacking. Pugliese takes De Caro's ideas and clothes them in humanity. He breathes life into them.

If we do the same thing for 1948's "**Boedo**" the comparison is less straightforward. Pugliese's recording is lighter on its feet than any of De Caro's four versions but it's also no longer typical of his output. It doesn't really have much in common with the tango on the other side of the record, which was "**Negracha**". Pugliese has succeeded in rescuing De Caro's inheritance and has moved on: we are now in the era of ***la yumba***.

These 1940s Pugliese instrumentals remain relatively unknown in many milongas, to the point that when you play them as a DJ people come and ask you what they were. (I really hope that I have to correct this statement by the time the second edition of this book comes out). The music demands your absolute presence – it calls forth in the dancers the same passion and integrity that it evinces. One *milonguero* who teaches in Europe once told me that he liked always to accept invitations to dance unless Pugliese was playing. For that, everything had to be just right.

All Pugliese's 1940s instrumentals are good, but there are two I would particularly wish to point you towards: "**Flor de tango**" and "**Derecho viejo**". These tangos exhibit an astonishing aggression in the violin section: one can almost see the horse-hairs flying off the bows of Julio Carrasco and Oscar Herrero as they disintegrate under the force of their attack. It's almost impossible to hear the violin played like this nowadays.

As we move into the 1950s Pugliese's music becomes even more intense. The instrumentals form an unbroken series of five star masterpieces, even as the vocal performances take a direction that is more difficult for us to appreciate today. As with the 40s material, this music is much broader than one might expect from the fare served up at the milongas. To give just one example, the *milonguero* Eduardo Aguirre used to love dancing to the Pugliese version of "**A los amigos**", but I don't think I ever heard it played except when he asked for it. My own passion reaches a maximum with tracks from 1950 such as the electrifying "**De floreo**".

As we move in to the 1960s, we enter a period in which tango had been supplanted in the public's affections by other kinds of music, especially rock and roll. It was difficult to keep a tango orchestra together. In October 1968, during a period when Pugliese was ill and thus unable to organise work for his orchestra, six of Pugliese's core musicians started working together as a sextet. It was not long before they had split from the maestro – on good terms, but it must nevertheless have been a terrible blow: the group included his first bandoneón Osvaldo Ruggiero who had been with him since 1939, his bass player Alcides Rossi (the son of his original bass player Aniceto Rossi) as well as the violinist Oscar Herrero. Their departure cut the heart out of the orchestra.

Pugliese reformed his orchestra in short order; gauge for yourself if he did so successfully by listening to one of the new orchestra's first recordings, the much loved "**A Evaristo Carriego**" (1969).

That's the end of our rough guide, and I hope I've convinced you (if you needed convincing) that a world of treasures is waiting for anyone who takes the time to explore this music. What's more, you can find most of it fairly easily nowadays, although the repression that Pugliese experienced from the authorities means that there are not so many of them: he was only permitted to record 10 discs a year, when his popularity merited many more. Amongst the losses, there is no 1940s version of the tango "**Recién**", Pugliese's own composition. We have to make do with the admittedly wonderful version of Tanturi with Campos, but can you imagine it recorded by Pugliese with Chanel?

	Tango	**Lyric**	**Recorded by**
1942	El encopao	Enrique Dizeo	Troilo; Rodríguez
1943	Recién	Homero Manzi	Láurenz; Tanturi
1945	Igual que una sombra	Enrique Cadícamo	Miguel Caló

Pugliese: the unrecorded tracks

I could go on about the many wonderful recordings of this orchestra, but I think it's better that you explore it yourselves. One note of caution: if you listen to this music, I mean, really listen to it, it's hard to listen to very much at a time. It really puts you through the wringer. Maybe we should give the same warning that you get with certain medicines: if you are affected by this music, do not attempt to drive or operate heavy machinery.

Pugliese on CD: what to listen to

We've already got 'Ausencia' and the four disc set 'Edición Aniversario'. Concentrate on the 1940s material and the 1950s instrumentals. The tracks with Jorge Vidal you can find on 'Sus cantores de los '50', which does not have as nice a cover as the CD on Magenta but does introduce you to one of his successors in the Pugliese orchestra, Juan Carlos Cobos.

Reliquias	499962	Instrumentales inolvidables vol.3	1999
Reliquias	499985	Instrumentales inolvidables vol.2	1999
Reliquias	495374	Sus éxitos con Roberto Chanel	1998
Reliquias	541703	Cantan Alberto Morán y Roberto Chanel	2002
Reliquias	837407	A los amigos	1996
Reliquias	529108	Sus cantores de los '50	2000
Reliquias	859023	Instrumentales inolvidables	1997

'Reliquias' also have two albums of Pugliese with Alberto Morán – you don't need those straight away, but dedicated collectors will end up buying them for the few great tracks they contain.

The 1960s recordings were on the Polygram label. Unless you're very keen on these, just get this compilation:

Polygram	539332	Nostálgico	1997

26/ The forgotten Troilo

Listening guide

ORQUESTA ANÍBAL TROILO

1/ Malena (1942) canta: Fiorentino

2/ Cotorrita de la suerte (1945) canta: Marino

3/ Sur (1948) canta: Edmundo Rivero

4/ Responso (1951) 5/ Tanguango (1951)

CUARTETO TROILO-GRELA

6/ Palomita blanca (v) (1953)

7/ La trampera (m) (1962)

Nearly all artists have periods when their work is stronger or weaker. Of the artists we have spoken about in this book, that would be true of all of them except perhaps Di Sarli, and his work would no doubt have suffered had he survived into the 1960s, as Pugliese's did.

From the perspective of the dancer these differences between strong and weak periods are amplified, because there is music which our brains tell us is good but to which our bodies don't wish to dance. The artist for whom this is most true is Aníbal Troilo. Revered in Argentina as one of the all-time greats, it is a very rare milonga, even in Buenos Aires, where one hears anything (save for a few of his valses) except the sides with Fiorentino – and of these, what gets played is just the up-tempo tracks from 1941. A recording career of thirty-three years is reduced to nine months.

There are good reasons for this: Troilo's music is sophisticated, and it requires skilful dancers – good listeners – to interpret his music. In the 1940s, Troilo gave more emphasis to the melody with each passing year; if the dancers cannot follow this, they will become lost. It also requires confident, discerning and skilful DJs to play this music: reserving it for a more experienced crowd, and even then choosing the right moment, as well as the right tracks.

Having said all this: we can do it! We can listen to, enjoy and dance to lots more of this music than we do normally.

Let's start with Fiorentino. Haven't we already covered him? No we haven't, because we're all stuck on the 1941 recordings. The 1942 material sounds surprisingly different: for instance the Troilo version of the Demare classic "**Malena**", or "**El encopao**" which we associate with Enrique Rodríguez.

Now let's move on to **Alberto Marino** who joined Troilo in 1943 as the second singer to Fiorentino. I've only once heard his music at a milonga and it wasn't in my own country. Can it really be true that his recordings are undanceable? It's a nonsense, of course. Let's listen to 1945's "**Cotorrita de la suerte**". The first thing you

notice – before the entrance of Marino – is the dynamic of the music: it starts very quietly and grows in strength. This use of the dynamic – typical for Troilo – is the first problem in any non-traditional milongas: the environment is just too noisy for people to hear properly. That's why we don't talk as much in the milonga as at a café: we are listening to this beautiful music!

The supreme example of a tango that suffers from these kinds of difficulties would be 1948's "**Sur**". This is revered as one of the finest compositions in the entire history of tango. Troilo wrote the music himself but the piece is remembered for the exquisite lyric by Homero Manzi. The musician Raúl Garello named "**Sur**" as his favourite tango and quoted the Argentine author Ernesto Sabato as having said that he'd exchange everything he had ever written to be the author of its lyric[18].

Unless you are a tango aficionado you've probably never heard of this tango because it is never played in the milonga. Edmundo Rivero's base-baritone is magisterial. In the final chorus, he drops his voice to the faintest whisper, accompanied only by the most gentle trembling of violins. I can only imagine what it must have been like to listen to this live: the entire room in rapt attention, Rivero with the audience in the palm of his hand, floating his words out into a silence which allows every nuance of his interpretation to be heard. It is a sublime moment, but one you can't hear today above the chatter of the crowd, or even the whirr of the air-conditioning.

Troilo changed style in 1950, allowing himself to experiment freely. Piazzolla is the main arranger and the results are quite daring. Some of it is outstanding. Why don't we hear it?

This time there's a different problem: at the same time as changing style, Troilo changed his record company, leaving RCA Victor for the now defunct Argentine label **TK**. The materials which TK used

[18] Raúl Garello, "Sur" in the Pagina 12, 6th May 2007. Available online at http://www.pagina12.com.ar/diario/suplementos/radar/17-3805-2007-05-06.html (accessed:24th June 2012)

for both their masters and their discs were of inferior quality and the records have not lasted as well as RCA Victor's: the fidelity of the records is noticeably poorer than that from the 1940s. TK ceased trading in 1963 but not before granting a limited license to Music Hall who made some LPs. All the transfers you hear today are from those LPs. No-one seems to know if the masters survived and it's not clear who owns the rights. I like to think they are locked in a vault somewhere, waiting to be discovered, but maybe that's just wishful thinking.

Now, after all this drama, what about the music? It's outstanding! Troilo has some magnificent new compositions such as "**Responso**", his response to the death of his close friend Homero Manzi (collaborator with Troilo on "**Sur**", "**Barrio de tango**", "**Romance de barrio**" and other enduring works). There are sensational versions of compositions by the new wave such as Salgán's "**A fuego lento**"; Alfredo Gobbi's "**Orlando Goñi**", a tribute to Troilo's lost pianist.; and of course Piazzolla arrangements of some of his own new work, such as "**Triunfal**". Troilo also tackles some *guardia vieja* classics which we don't think of as belonging to his repertoire, such as "**Fuegos artificales**", "**Ojos negros**" and "**El pollo Ricardo**". These are wonderful performances and the most danceable of his 1950s output, which is not afraid to use *rubato* (the stretching of musical time).

Finally there is the most incredible experimental number with drums – not a drum kit, but tambors, the drums used in *candombe* – that makes Canaro's novelty numbers sound pretty conservative. The result is "**Tanguango**" and the first time most people hear it, it blows their socks off!

The 1950s also saw the beginning of Troilo's collaboration with the guitarist Roberto Grela in a quartet. Grela was the finest guitarist of his generation and in this format Troilo – thought by many to be the greatest bandoneón player ever – could give free rein to his superb bandoneón playing in a way that was simply not possible in the orchestra. The group met only for recordings and made only two LPs: one on TK in the 1950s (12 tracks) and one on RCA Victor in 1962 (12 tracks). It's hard not to recommend everything – the quality really is that good – but try the vals "**Palomita blanca**" and the milonga "**La trampera**".

In 1957 Troilo joined Odeón, recording 24 tracks with them by the end of the decade. There are only five instrumentals, but they are fascinating because they present the best balance between musicality and fidelity. What do I mean? Well, the fidelity of the sound is really very good – very clean and dynamic, if not quite as detailed as the stereo recordings Troilo would make in the 1960s. The trouble with those later recordings is that people aren't dancing anymore, and you can hear it. Plenty of people have the Troilo instrumental album in the series 'RCA Victor 100 Años' which presents those 60s recordings and never play it. The sound fidelity is outstanding, but it is a symphonic tango and our bodies are not moved. As dancers, we might have decided that these final recordings are not for us, but the rest is unjustly forgotten.

The forgotten Troilo: what to listen to

For the 1940s output, listen to the rest of the albums in BMG's series '**Aníbal Troilo en RCA Victor**' – but take it slowly. This is not fast-food: it takes time to savour. It will very likely be many years into your tango life before you start appreciating this music. The process is perhaps similar to that of becoming a connoisseur of fine whisky.

BMG	659438	Barrio de tango (1942)	2004
BMG	659439	Uno (1943)	2004
BMG	659440	La cumparsita (1943)	2004
BMG	659441	Tres amigos (1944)	2004
BMG	659442	Quejas de bandoneón (1944)	2004
BMG	659443	María (1945)	2004
BMG	659444	Adiós pampa mía (1945/1946)	2004
BMG	659445	Mientras gime el bandoneón (1946)	2004
BMG	659446	Romance de barrio (1946/1947)	2004
BMG	659447	Cafetín de Buenos Aires (1948/1949)	2004

The 1950s material is easier to digest but I'm guessing you won't want to listen to all of it. For this reason I'm recommending the Lantower album, which is a kind of Troilo 1950s Greatest Hits, even though Euro have better transfers.

For Troilo-Grela, Euro have both the 1950s tracks from TK and the 1962 album on RCA Victor, so there's no need to get the album on BMG which only has the later material.

Euro	14033	Troilo – Grela	2010
Lantower	81047	Grandes del Tango 39 – Aníbal Troilo 4	2007

Part 5

Tango Stories

27 / I don't know what your eyes have done to me: The tragic and unforgettable story of Francisco Canaro & Ada Falcón

Listening guide

ORQUESTA FRANCISCO CANARO

1/ Sentimiento gaucho (1930)

2/ Yo no sé qué me han hecho tus ojos (v) (1930)

3/ No mientas! (1938)

4/ Nada más (1938)

ORQUESTA FRANCISCO CANARO
dir. Roberto Garza

5/ Corazón encadenado (1942)

In the 1920s and early 1930s, tango – the popular music of its day – was a huge phenomenon in the theatre and there were many famous singers who didn't work with dance orchestras but were rather stars of the stage and screen. Of those stars, we now tell the story of Ada Falcón.

Ada was a beautiful young woman with a strong personality. When our story opens in 1929 she was already very successful in her own right. She had been pushed onto the stage by her ambitious mother at the age of five. Thanks to the help of the pianist Enrique Delfino, who had heard her performing on stage, she already had her own contract, bringing her fame, wealth, and independence. She lived a life of luxury, with a huge house in the up-market district of Palermo, fast cars, and the attention of a string of rich and powerful admirers. One of them, a Maharaja, gave her a solitaire diamond and tried to abduct her. Amidst all these distractions however she had found love with a young politician, Carlos Washington Lencinas.

Now when I say beautiful, Ada was simply stunning, and with a voice to match. If you want to know, watch her singing "**Sentimiento gaucho**" in the 1934 Argentine film "Idolos de la Radio". The look on Ignacio Corsini's face when her hears the power of her voice could be the look of any of us, hearing the majesty, richness and drama of this voice for the first time. Ada is completely captivating; her performance is electrifying. Listen to this remarkable lyric, which could have come from the mouth of Buddha:

> *Know this: the condition of man is suffering*
>
> - lyric of "Sentimiento gaucho" (Juan Andrés Caruso)

In 1929, Francisco Canaro was a very successful and famous orchestra leader – and a married man. With his finger on the pulse of the public mood, Canaro had already invited Ada to record with him.

In November of that year Ada's boyfriend Carlos Washington Lencinas was assassinated. She wrote a song in his memory,

"**Sueño con el**" ("I dream of him") which Canaro and Ada recorded together. One thing led to another, and they embarked on a passionate affair which was lived out very much in the public eye. Today we would call them a celebrity couple.

The astonishing thing about this story is that we can follow it through the songs they recorded together, particularly if we pay attention to the songs in which one or other of them wrote the lyric. They recorded 201 numbers together over a period of thirteen years. The first was "**Aquel tapado de armiño**" ("That Mink Coat"). The lyric of this tango deals with the expensive gift of a mink coat and the consequences that ensue. Whilst, in May 1929, Ada Falcón is still happily with another man, one can't help but feel that this prefigures what is to come.

In 1930, Canaro and Falcón recorded a vals which Canaro had just written: "**Yo no se que me han hecho tus ojos**" ("I don't know what your eyes have done to me"). Ada was famous for her large and beautiful green eyes, and there's no doubt what this song is about. This is an offering, a love song written for Ada by Canaro.

Imagine the scene in the recording studio as she sings those words to him, which he has written. Or when, the same year, she sings Canaro's tango, "**Vos también tenés tu historia**" ("You've got your history as well")?

Ada wanted Canaro to divorce, but Canaro, rich as he was, would not countenance losing half of his money. Canaro's wife (whom Ada nicknamed "la francesa") was having none of it. She did her best to frighten Ada off, stalking her, even scratching her cars.

Things came to a head one day in 1938 when Canaro's wife decided to go to the recording studio. In a break between takes, Ada and Canaro had retired to a small office. Ada was sitting in Canaro's lap. Suddenly, the door burst open. "La francesa" appeared in the doorway, opened her handbag and drew a gun, pointing it at Ada, who fled.

Feigning illness, Ada cancelled her concert appearances and confined herself to her home, withdrawing from public life. She agreed to honour her recording contracts only if she could sing behind a curtain, so that no-one could see her. Once these responsibilities were discharged she became more and more of a recluse, leaving the house only to go to Mass with her mother.

Canaro's response was to start another affair – some say with Ada's sister Adhelma.

The recorded numbers tell the story. Her last studio date with Canaro is in 1938, when she sings four numbers. Two of them are

"**No mientas**" – "Don't lie" – and "**Nada más**" – "Nothing more".

I find that modern audiences, especially outside the Latin world, often have trouble taking tango lyrics seriously. They find them over the top, and in a way it's true – this is the operatic influence brought to Argentina by the Italians. But: the story of difficulty in love is everyone's story. You would think that modern man and woman had never had a broken heart or loved someone they shouldn't have. Listen to these lyrics, which Falcón sings to Canaro that day, for the very last time:

> I want nothing, nothing more
> Just don't leave me, face to face with life
> I'll die if you leave me
> Because without you I don't know how to live

After all this you would think that Ada Falcón had suffered enough, but no; there is more to come.

In 1940 a new man entered Ada's life, the glamorous Mexican actor and singer José Mojica who was in Buenos Aires to act in the film "Melodias da Americas". They seemed to have a lot in common: both were successful and beautiful, both religious, both very close to their mothers. They began a romantic liaison. Perhaps Ada could find love again?

It was not to be. One day, Ada walked into José's dressing room to find him in the arms of another man.

This final betrayal seems to have unhinged Ada. She left the house only to go to church, dressed entirely in black. There she shouted aloud at the statues, begging for forgiveness. Finally she had a vision of Saint Francis, and she made the decision to retire to a Franciscan convent in Cordoba.

Before leaving, she recorded two more numbers with Canaro's orchestra but, doubtless on her insistence, without Canaro. For the occasion it was led by the arranger Roberto Garza.

The numbers she chose for her final recordings were: "**Corazón encadenado**" ("Heart in chains") and "**Viviré con tu recuerdo**" ("I will live with your memory").

Sixty years later, an Argentine researcher tracked her down and she granted him an interview which you can see in the astonishing documentary "**Yo no se que me han hecho tus ojos**". This interview tears at your heart. Asked outright whether she and Canaro were in love, she cries "No! No! No… no…" and you know it means, yes.

Ada died on the 4th January, 2002 and was buried in Buenos Aires at the Chacarita cemetery. Only six people attended her funeral.

She is interred in the same mausoleum as Canaro.

Acknowledgement:
Nada Más (tango). Music: Juan D'Arienzo. Lyric: Luis Rubinstein.
Published by Warner/Chappell Music Argentina
Lyric by kind permission of SADAIC

28 / Emperor Hirohito offered to send a submarine: the tango in Japan

Although tango faded in importance outside Argentina after the war and was sinking towards oblivion in Argentina in the 1970s, there was one country where it remained popular: Japan.

The story of how Tango arrived in Japan is an important one, because it reveals how the Japanese became such avid record collectors.

Tango came to Japan from Paris (where else) in 1926. It was brought home by Baron "Tsunami" Megata, the son of a diplomat, who had spent six years in Paris. Having travelled there for a hip operation, he recovered by learning to dance tango at the cabaret "El Garrón".

Megata returned home with a large stack of records from all the most important orchestras of the day and opened a tango academy offering free tango lessons for the Japanese aristocracy. Tango became more and more popular, and by the time Juan Canaro (one of Francisco Canaro's brothers) arrived in 1954 there were already more than twenty Japanese *orquestas típica.* Francisco himself arrived in 1961.

There was one orchestra that the Japanese specially wanted to welcome to their country, that of Juan D'Arienzo, but D'Arienzo was reluctant to make the long journey. Matters reached the highest level of the Japanese government, and in 1968 Emperor Hirohito intervened personally. He sent a blank cheque to D'Arienzo via the Japanese embassy in Buenos Aires, inviting D'Arienzo to name the sum for him and his orchestra.

However, D'Arienzo was frightened of flying. His close friend Carlos Gardel had tragically died in an aeroplane accident in Columbia in 1935. Gardel would often come to hear D'Arienzo play at the Chantecler Cabaret, and D'Arienzo claimed that Gardel had once said to him[19]:

> *"Look, Juanito, I think I'm going to die in a plane!"*
> *I answered him, "Stop that nonsense! Don't talk bullshit." But it was not nonsense. He foresaw it.*

Hirohito was informed that D'Arienzo would not fly, but he was not to be put off. He offered to send a warship. Hearing that the journey would take forty days, D'Arienzo refused this as well. Finally, Hirohito offered to send a submarine, which would cut fifteen days off the journey. This too was refused on the grounds that he would be isolated on the journey and unable to get off: what if Japan decided to enter a war whilst he was en route?

In the end the orchestra went without him. Pianist Juan Polito led the orchestra for the tour, which was so successful that they returned in 1970.

---

[19] La Maga magazine, Buenos Aires, Wednesday January 13, 1993.

29/ Osvaldo Pugliese: Al Colón!

Listening guide

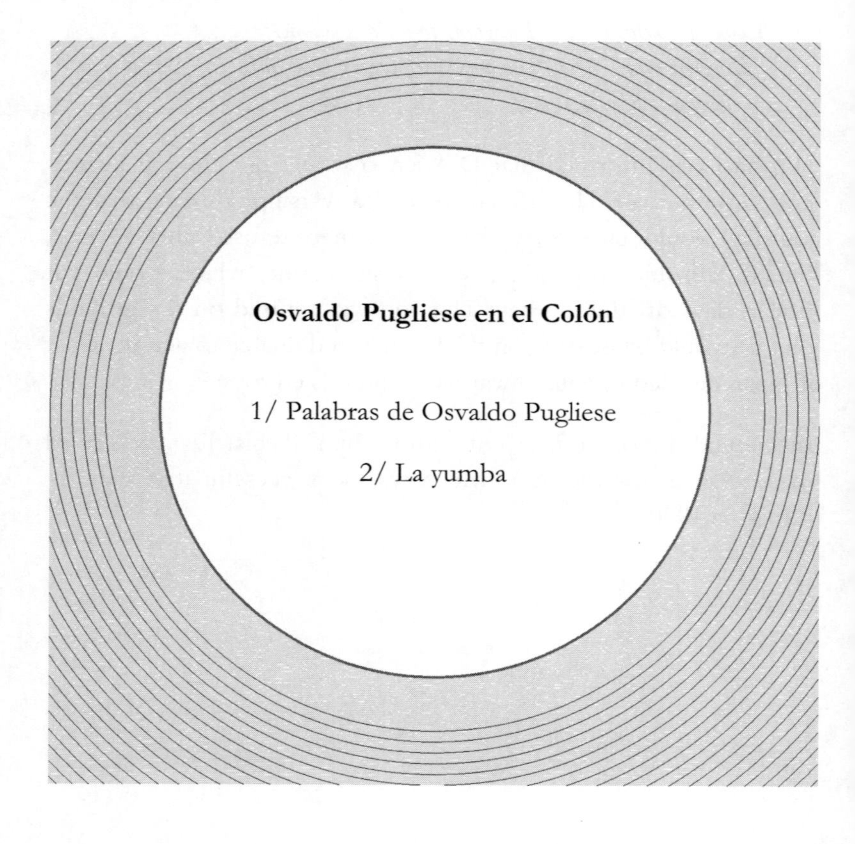

In 1948, the Osvaldo Pugliese orchestra appeared in the Argentine film "Mis cinco hijos". Three tracks appear in full. The scene takes place in a milonga, with dancing couples and a crowd of fans at the foot of the stage. As the orchestra plays the final chord of "**La yumba**", the fans break into wild applause and shout: Al Colón!

Now the Teatro Colón is the principal theatre and opera house in Buenos Aires. It is no provincial affair. Designed to be more opulent than the famous La Scala in Milan, this is the most luxurious theatre in the southern hemisphere and is considered one of the finest theatres in the world. Among the great artists who have appeared there are Strauss, Caruso, Maria Callas, Anna Pavlova, Nijinsky, Baryshnikov, Margot Fonteyn, Toscanini, Furtwängler and Pavarotti to name just a few.

Al Colón! – meaning, To the Colón! – expresses the hope of Pugliese's fans that their hero, a working class man and lifelong communist, a man hounded by the police and frequently imprisoned, will appear on the same stage as these greats in the theatre that has been called the "temple of the oligarchy".

Clearly it's a joke.

Nevertheless, as we know, life loves a jest.

In 1985, the military regime in Argentina had been toppled by the disastrous adventure of the Falklands war, and the country was experimenting with a new freedom. Somehow it was arranged for Osvaldo Pugliese – now in his 80th year – to give a concert in the Teatro Colón.

The concert was filmed and so we can share in something of the atmosphere of that historic night, which as you can imagine was completely electric.

The theatre's website has a whole page listing the many great artists who have played there.

It does not mention Osvaldo Pugliese.

However let's leave the last words not to them but to the maestro who was brought to the microphone before the final number and asked to say a few words. With characteristic humility, he said:[20]

> *The truth is... it's a night of the people, of the masses, lovers of our genre, our beloved genre, tango.*
>
> *We are just a child of the tango machine, a screw of this machine, nothing more; at certain times we may be useful and other times not.*

Pugliese went on to thank the organisers and all the musicians who had laboured alongside him since 1939. Finally he dedicated the final number with these words:

> *This fulfils the dream of my beloved mother – I don't have her any longer – and if you'll allow me, I'd like to dedicate the next tango to my beloved mother; because she was the first one to say: "Al Colón".*

For the last number, "**La yumba**", Pugliese was joined on stage by many musicians who had played with him over the years, including **Osvaldo Ruggiero**, a veteran from the 1939 orchestra. In all, the line of bandoneóns extended to ten musicians.

They brought the house down.

Don Osvaldo received five standing ovations.

[20] transcribed from "Osvaldo Pugliese en el Teatro Colón 1985", VHS. The CD has the speech but part of it has been edited out.

Postscript

We need more words for sounds.

We live in a visual age. As I wrote this book I found myself struggling to find expressions and even words for experiences which are not visual in their nature. I spoke about a musician's *musical vision*, or explained how he changed the *musical landscape*. The chapters are *illustrated* by musical examples. We take an *overview* of someone's career, or take it in *at a glance*.

Sound does not work like this.

Sound has creative power.

My wish is that we may experience this with this music, our music, our beloved tango. Before the last notes die away, may it transform us.

Appendix: How to be a Tango DJ

Recently someone told me he wanted to be a Tango DJ. I asked him, why? He thought for a moment and replied: "When I dance, I feel things in the music… I want to share this".

Yes! In my opinion, this is the best reason for becoming a Tango DJ: to share your passion for the music. Let's say that again: **to be a tango DJ is to share your passion for tango music with other people**.

This leads us directly to the first rule of being a tango DJ.

Rule 1: only play what you like

Taste is personal. Let's face it: there will be good music that everyone likes that you don't like yourself. Here's a personal example. The world adores Glenn Gould's performances of Bach's Goldberg variations. Personally, I can't stand Gould's relentless mechanical hammering: I wish he'd just played a harpsichord instead. This doesn't mean that one opinion or the other has to be correct. Who knows, maybe one day someone will change my mind, and open my ears to the beauty of his playing. In the meantime, it means that, at an evening of classical music, I could not play one of Glenn Gould's Goldberg variations. It would go against my inner feeling for the music. What then could I share?

Rule 2: don't play anything bad

There's a lot of tango music. Not all of it is good to play in the milonga. I have lost count of how many evenings I have been to which were sabotaged by the DJ trying too hard to impress, playing novelties that just don't work. Don't do it!

Okay, so being a DJ is much more than these first two things – but many people never get past these first two. Just obeying these first two rules lets you assemble a playlist in *tandas* that will keep most people happy.

Rule 3: play your music in tandas

A *tanda* is a set of music that has a similar feeling. The purpose of a *tanda* is to allow you to sink more deeply into the music. Shorter *tandas* create more energy; longer *tandas* create more depth. Typically a *tanda* will be 3 or 4 songs long, depending on the length of the evening, the genre (tango, vals, milonga) and of course the DJ. My own preference is to have tango *tandas* of 4 rather than 3 songs unless the community is young and the evening short.

A typical cycle of *tandas* of tango (T), vals (V) and milonga (M) will run like this:

T-T-V-T-T-M

The *cortina* or curtain tune (the word literally means curtain) is a piece of music that signals that the *tanda* is over. It takes its name from the days when the stage curtain would be lowered whilst one orchestra was changed for another.

In a traditional milonga, the *cortina* has the function of clearing the floor, enabling people to choose new partners for the new music.

In a non-traditional setting you don't have to use *cortinas* but it can still be very useful for people to know when the *tanda* is over. It's also essential at festivals or anywhere where the dancers are not predominantly from only one community, so cannot know how long the *tandas* usually are.

The *cortina* affects the mood of the evening and allows the DJ to communicate with the audience. My main preparation for a big milonga is choosing the *cortina(s)*, which I may only ever use once.

The *cortina* also allows you to make bigger contrasts between one tanda and the next. It acts as a palette cleanser between courses, like a sorbet.

It's best if your *cortina* isn't danceable. Picking cortinas is quite an art, and a different skill to selecting tango music. You want people to remember your *cortina*, but if it draws more attention than your tango music – something is not quite right.

It can be useful as well if you fade the *cortina* out yourself rather than having a "pre-faded" *cortina* because then you can vary the length of the *cortina* during the evening – shorter at the beginning, longer when the room fills up. In a traditional milonga this doesn't matter – the *cortina* will run for a minute until the floor is completely empty, and nobody minds. Also pay attention to the volume – it can be disturbing if the *cortina* is louder than the rest of the music. This is especially important at events such as marathons where one is trying to encourage a deeper flow.

These first three rules can take you a long way, but three more take us deeper into the art of tango DJ-ing.

Rule 4: Don't rely on a fixed playlist

Oh yes! Whilst it's possible to arrive with a playlist, particularly for a familiar event with a familiar crowd, you have to be able to react to the floor. Even your first *tanda* may have to fit in with the lesson which is just finishing.

It's much harder to come with a playlist when you don't know the community. For instance, will you be able to play Pugliese? You just don't know in advance.

Rule 5: watch the floor

If everyone is sitting down, time to play something else.

If the room is chaotic, time to play something calming.

If the energy is low, time to spice things up.

In other words, the DJ has to have a lot of attention on the dance floor. He can't just hole himself up in what some have called the "DJ bunker".

Rule 6: know your music – don't rely on pre-listening

You'll sometimes see the DJ with headphones on, listening to something different than what is currently playing. We call this pre-listening. This has its uses but as a DJ your attention needs to be with your audience. You simply don't have time to trawl through your library looking for new ideas. Pre-listening is more limited. It's for identifying the tune that you've got in your head but whose title you've forgotten, or to check certain things about tanda construction.

Tanda construction

Up to a point you can throw three or four songs of a certain orchestra together from a similar period and it will work as a tanda. However there is more than this to constructing a good tanda. For instance, considering the pace and energy of the tanda, will it be flat, rising, falling (rare) or hammock shaped (dipping in the middle)? *Tandas* of three generally work best with an even or rising energy; with a tanda of four, you can have a dip in the middle, especially with the third song – this is the place to try out a new song you are not sure about.

Furthermore there are songs which are definitely first songs or last songs. For instance, some songs have such a definite ending that you just have to put them at the end of the tanda. They create a musical full stop, and everyone will feel like sitting down afterwards.

Conversely there are some songs that need to go at the beginning of a tanda, mostly songs with a clear introduction (although sometimes you can edit these out).

Then there are songs which cannot go in the middle of a tanda because they are simply too famous. One example would be Canaro's "**Poema**". This works best as an opener – please don't play it too often!

What about mixing vocals and instrumentals in one tanda, or mixing vocalists?

To answer this kind of question, imagine that we could go back in time to 1941 and listen to the Troilo orchestra at its absolute peak. We are dancing to an instrumental number. They begin their next, but just before the minute mark Fiorentino, immaculately dressed in a white tuxedo, strolls up to the microphone, arriving right on cue. We didn't even know he was going to sing in this number. Does it disturb us? No, it delights us! Providing the energy of the pieces fits together well I think this is just fine.

Match the mood – watch the year

Much more important is matching the mood, and a huge part of that is determined by the year in which a tango was recorded. Music from the 1930s is very different to music from the early 40s, or the late 40s, or the 50s. Or the 70s. You can work intuitively or you can tag your music with the recording year – or both. However, if your feeling for music is shall we say still young, then you had better rely on your tags. Please don't play the 1971 D'Arienzo "**La cumparsita**" with "**El flete**" (1936), just because you gave them both 5 stars in iTunes.

Tango music is boring, can you play some "tango nuevo" or "neotango"

This is a non-Argentine problem brought on by a very narrow idea of what goes on in a "traditional" milonga. In Argentina this cycle of music is broken up by *tandas* of what they call "*tropical*" – mostly cumbias of various descriptions – and sometimes swing. This extrovert music injects some pace and energy and keeps things lively. Outside Argentina such *tandas* may well clear the floor because many tango dancers don't dance anything else. The DJ has to work harder to keep the music feeling fresh.

And finally… never forget that a milonga is a party!

Glossary

arrastre: originally a bandoneón effect, keying the note before you start to open the bellows, accelerating towards the beat and stopping suddenly with a little rebound. This effect can be reproduced on the other instruments.

bandoneón: the dark toned bisonic button accordion originating in Germany that gives tango music its characteristic sonority.

bandoneonista: a player of the **bandoneón**.

cadencia: swing or cadence – not simply a musical term in tango.

candombe: the major dance and music of the black communities in Argentina and especially Uruguay. Traditionally the music was just drums and the genre has obvious African roots.

canta (plural **cantan**): literally, sings. The Argentine way of saying, "vocals by".

cantor de orquesta: orchestra singer – the name given to the singer of a dance orchestra who is singing the full lyric, as opposed to an *estribillista*. He (and it's always a man) is identified with the 1940s.

canyengue: an untranslatable word! Something like "duende" in Spanish, or "swing" in jazz. It means, first of all, street-wise or sassy; done with flair. Next, it refers to a very old style of dancing tango from the first decade of the 20th century, leaning forwards with bent knees, in a V embrace and with the holding hands held down at the waist. Thirdly it is a rhythm, a kind of syncopation.

chicharra: playing on the string wrappers on the violin to make a percussive, scratching sound.

compás: the musical beat or pulse, often compared to a heartbeat. Not the same thing as rhythm, which may be more complex.

estribillista: a singer of the *estribillo (q.v.)*, or refrain singer for short – chorus singer can mean something else in English!

estribillo: the refrain or chorus.

glosa: a lyric poem designed to be declaimed over tango music. Very few were recorded; the most famous example is D'Agostino's "**Café Dominguez**".

glosador: a reader of *glosas.*

guardia vieja: the *old guard* – the old timers, who played tango the old fashioned way.

látigo *(music)*: literally, whip, this is the Argentine way of talking about *glissando* (sliding) on the violin.

legato *(music)*: smooth, with the adjacent notes connected together.

lunfardo: the porteño *(q.v)* argot with many words from European dialects.

marcato: "marked": a musical term meaning accented – normally with a sharp attack that falls away.

milonga: originally: the *milonga campera (q.v.)* and also a place where you went to dance. Only later did this come to mean a separate dance style. Nowadays people talk about **milonga lisa**, literally smooth milonga, to distinguish it from the rougher **milonga con traspié**. Simply speaking, *milonga lisa* is not syncopated.

milonga campera: a folk music from Argentina with a rhythm closely related to the Cuban habanera. The *milonga campera* was never danced, but was an important ingredient in the early tango.

milonguero/milonguera: a man (milonguero) or woman (milonguera) whose life is formed around being at the milonga, someone with tango *en las venas* – in the blood.

obligato *(music)*: a variation on counter melody that is so essential to the music that one is obliged to play it.

porteño: an inhabitant of the port, i.e. Buenos Aires. Feminine form: *porteña.*

ritmo: the rhythm – important, but nothing without *compás (q.v.).*

rubato *(music)*: changing the pace of the music in a free way, without a clear tempo – used a great deal by Pugliese and also Troilo from the 1950s onwards.

salón: a dance hall.

staccato *(music)*: choppy, made from short notes that have a space in between.

tango-canción: a tango meant for singing rather than for dancing.

tango-milonga: originally this simply meant a tango for dancing, as opposed to *tango-canción.* At the time this term was being used, back in the 1910s and 1920s, tango music was relatively undeveloped and the rhythm was basically the primitive milonga rhythm. The term has thus come to refer to tangos with the feeling of this period.

tango de salón: not really a style of dance at all, but simply means tango that's danced in a dance hall rather than in the street (or on stage).

traspié: many use this word today to mean double time in milonga, but that's not what it means. Traspié comes from *tras-pied*, across (*tras*) the foot (*pied*), i.e. to *stumble.* It refers to a particular way of using syncopated double time in milonga with changes of direction.

vals: the Spanish word for waltz. Among tango aficionados, it's a shorthand for tango-vals, the style of vals performed in the salons of Buenos Aires.

variación (music): a variation, normally used as the climax of the piece, much like a cadenza in classical music. This is the chance for some virtuoso playing in one of the instruments, often the bandoneón.